DEATH TO THE KING

The Story of the English Civil War

Since the signing of Magna Carta in 1215, the English had sought to limit the power of the Crown. Some four centuries later the well-meaning but shortsighted Charles I, a believer in absolute monarchy, defied Parliament and tried to rule without it. By 1640, however, after disastrous wars in Europe and Scotland, he found he could not do so without the tax money only Parliament could raise. But this new Parliament— the Long Parliament—was as determined to reassert the tradition of basic English rights as the King was to bend it to his wishes. Finally, the King and the Cavalier army faced the Puritan forces led by a previously obscure man named Oliver Cromwell in a civil war that not only shaped the future of England, but profoundly influenced the world. Refusing to recognize that even kings could not hold themselves above the law, Charles I became the tragic victim of the forces of history and his own outworn ideals.

Death to the King

The Story of the English Civil War

by Clifford Lindsey Alderman

Map and Drawings

Published by
BAILEY BROTHERS AND SWINFEN LTD.
FOLKESTONE

For Marian Jordan

Printed in Great Britain by
Lewis Reprints Ltd.
member of Brown Knight & Truscott Group
London and Tonbridge

Contents

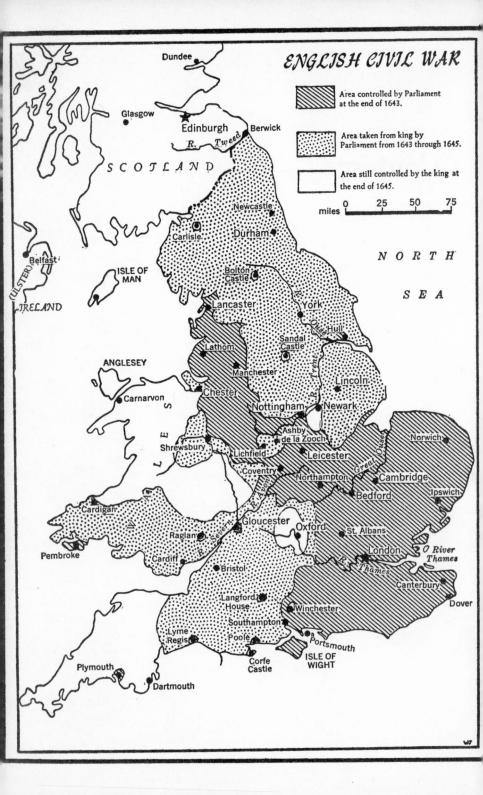

1

The Block

It was still dark in London as the watchmen making their rounds bawled, "Past five o'clock on a cold, snowy morning!" Bitterly cold it was on this 30th day of January, 1649. Tradesmen who had to be early at their work stomped briskly through the narrow streets, swinging their arms. Their breath, coming rapidly, turned to misty clouds as they exhaled. The snowfall was light but steady.

In his apartment at St. James's Palace, the King was still sleeping quite peacefully. On a pallet beside his bed, his faithful servant Herbert was wakeful, however; indeed, he had scarcely closed an eye through a night that seemed endless.

At half past five the King woke. "I will get up now," he said to the servant, "for I have a great work to do today. I would be as trim today as may be."

It must be very cold outside, he knew, for royal palaces in those days were drafty, and the fire on the hearth could not dispel the chill that seeped into the chamber. For that reason the King chose the clothing he would wear with an eye to its warmth.

"I will not have the people see me shiver in the cold lest they think me afraid," he told Herbert.

He put on two linen shirts. Over them went a waistcoat of rich, red-striped silk, brocaded with silver and yellow. His doublet and breeches were of black satin. A short velvet cloak completed the costume. The only ornaments the King wore were earrings, each a pearl surmounted by a small gold crown, and the blue ribbon, golden emblem and badge of the Order of the Garter.

Dressing and the King's painstaking toilet lasted an hour. For a year he had allowed his beard to grow. His chestnut-coloured hair was beginning to turn white, and this was especially noticeable in the full beard. Now he had Herbert trim it with the greatest attention.

These preparations completed, the King's old friend William Juxon, the Bishop of London, arrived to give him communion.

At about ten there was a gentle tap on the bedchamber door. Herbert paid no attention to it. Then came a sharp rapping. Still Herbert did not move until the King said, "Open the door."

A man in the scarlet uniform of a colonel in the Puritan army stood there. "I wish to speak to the King," he said.

"Let him come in," the King called out.

Colonel Hacker entered. He was trembling a little. "It is time to go to Whitehall, sir."

"Go outside and wait for me," said the King. "I will be with you in a moment."

Hacker, Juxon and Herbert withdrew, leaving the King alone. He soon joined them. Taking the bishop by the hand, he smiled and said, "Come, let us be going."

To Colonel Hacker he remarked, "I am grateful for a walk on such a cold morning. It will restore my circulation."

Then all left the red-brick St. James's Palace by a door leading into the palace garden. The snow had stopped falling, but the gloomy sky still threatened.

They crossed the garden and went through a gate in the wall enclosing St. James's Park. No sooner had they passed through it than a deafening roll of drums began. Drawn up in a double line on each side of the path that ran across the park were companies of infantry armed with muskets. They were holding back the dense throng of spectators behind them.

The King had no clue to the feelings of those in the crowd about what they saw. He could see little of their faces behind the soldiers, and the thunder and crash of the drums drowned out any sound they may have made.

The onlookers pressed forward and craned their necks to get a better look. They saw a slight figure walking beside his escort. If, as he had feared, the King had shivered, they would have known it was only from the cold, for although his long face was melancholy, as it had always been, the gray eyes, surveying the people, held no trace of fear.

The bedlam in St. James's Park came from the drummers in a company of halberdiers leading the march—stalwart Puritan fighting men in steel helmets, carrying their sharp-pointed halberds with axlike heads. A second company swung into line behind the King and his escort.

The pace of the procession was slow. Perhaps the Puritan leaders had so ordered it to give the spectators a better look. At last the King called out to the halberdiers ahead of him: "March apace!" They quickened their step.

Suddenly, from the direction of St. James's Palace, a small dog scampered up, gamboling playfully at the King's heels. It was his favourite spaniel, Rogue. The little fellow had somehow managed to slip out of the palace, overjoyed at the prospect of a morning stroll with his master. Someone dived for him and bore him away. The King gave no sign that he saw.

Now Whitehall Palace loomed ahead. It sprawled for half a mile along the River Thames, an immense, untidy collection of buildings of all sizes, ages and types of architecture. Parts of it were very old, but King Henry VIII had built several additions in the Tudor style.

The procession was nearing the main entrance, known as the Holbein Gate. It was impressive, made of dull red brick, with two high turrets which had notched battlements around their tops.

At the gate the King ran nimbly up an outside staircase to a gallery which crossed over the gateway itself. From its windows he could look north up the thoroughfare called the Strand. It was black with people crowding toward the palace.

In the other direction, southward, lay Westminster Abbey and ancient Westminster Palace, where Parliament and the high courts of justice for the kingdom sat. Around these buildings clustered the dark, narrow alleys and ramshackle rookeries of one of London's worst slums. Today this area was deserted. Its poverty-stricken inhabitants—indeed, all in London who could possibly get away—were heading for Whitehall.

Already the rectangular space inside the Holbein Gate was jammed with people. Only the massed files of soldiers held them back from a platform just outside the magnificent building known as the Banqueting Hall. At each end of the area a troop of cavalry was drawn up. And from the windows of the gallery above the gate, the King could also see a host of spectators on the rooftops and at the windows of neighbouring buildings.

Inside the palace grounds he was taken through the long passage known as the Stone Gallery. Here hung the King's collection of masterpieces by the celebrated painters of the time, for he was a great lover and patron of art.

From the Stone Gallery, the King entered the building which housed the royal apartments. Here he was taken to await a summons. He hoped it would not be long in coming.

In an outer room of the apartments, a guard approached Colonel Tomlinson, in command of the Puritan troops there. "There is a man outside who demands to see the King," the soldier said.

"He cannot see the King," said Tomlinson.

"He says it is most urgent and refuses to go away," replied the guard.

"Where is he?"

"Walking up and down the Stone Gallery, sir."

Tomlinson went there. The man was Henry Seymour, who had once been page of honour to the King, When he told the Puritan officer his errand, Tomlinson took him straight to the royal apartments.

Entering the chamber where the King was, Seymour burst into a flood of tears. He knelt, kissed the King's hand and then clasped him about the legs in an agony of grief. Then he handed the King a letter from his son Charles, the heir to the English throne, who had sent this envoy from France with all possible speed.

The King read the letter slowly and carefully. For the first time his melancholy face was touched with a deeper sadness.

Enclosed with the letter was a sheet of paper. The only thing on it, at the very bottom, was the prince's signature.

Seymour then explained that a second copy of this paper

had been given to the Puritan leaders who now controlled England. They could fill in whatever they wished on the paper above the signature, he said.

"Your son will do anything, *anything*," Seymour added. "He will even give up his right of succession to the throne."

The King's smile made his dour face radiant. He threw the paper with his son's signature into the fire. Then he gave Seymour a letter he had already written—a message to his beloved son.

When Seymour was gone, there was a knock at the door. Bishop Juxon went outside. He was gone only an instant, and he said nothing when he returned. Then came a second knock. Once more the bishop went outside.

"It is the five Puritan ministers who offered their services to you before, your Majesty," he said when he came back.

"Send them away," said the King.

"I have already told them that, your Majesty, but they will not be satisfied. They insist on an answer from you."

"Then thank them for their offer," said the King, "but tell them plainly that they, who have so often prayed against me, shall never pray for me in this agony."

But as the bishop went to the door, the King changed his mind. "Tell them that they may if they please—and I will thank them for it—pray for me."

The bells of London were striking noon. A servant appeared to ask what the King would like for dinner.

"Nothing," he replied.

"But your Majesty," remonstrated Juxon, "no one can tell how long you must wait. In this bitter cold you might faint when you go out there."

The King nodded understandingly. "Perhaps a manchet and a glass of claret."

He ate half the manchet—a small loaf of white bread—
and drank the wine.

The faithful Herbert was still with his master, but now
he took Bishop Juxon aside. His face was ashen and he was
trembling. "I am afraid, your Reverence," he said. "I cannot
answer for my actions any longer." He held out a white
linen embroidered cap. "His Majesty ordered me to have this
ready, but I shall not be able to endure the sight of what
they will do to him."

Juxon took the cap. "I will see to that," he said. "You
can wait in the Banqueting Hall."

At last the long-awaited summons came. Juxon and
Herbert fell to their knees, weeping. The King gave his hand
to them. Tenderly, he helped the aged bishop to his feet.

Colonel Hacker and a guard of soldiers were at the
door. "Go on," said the King. "I will follow."

To reach its destination it was necessary for the procession to pass through the Banqueting Hall. Within the great
chamber were many soldiers of Oliver Cromwell's Puritan
army.

The King knew the place well. He had hired the famous
artist, Rubens, to do a magnificent series of paintings on the
ceiling. They showed the chief events of his father's reign,
his own birth, and finally his coming to the throne at his
father's death. Beneath it, in all its splendour and glory, the
King now passed.

Meanwhile, outside in the courtyard, the vast throng
waited impatiently. The cold bit savagely at their fingers and
toes. They could not even move about to get warm, so tightly
were they packed about the platform. Yet none would have
exchanged places with those who had come too late to squeeze
inside the courtyard.

As yet there was little to see. The wooden platform was built against the side of the Banqueting Hall. Its floor was even with the lower part of the windows on the first floor. Actually it was L-shaped, for it turned the corner around a little addition which had been built on the left end of the main building. There a window had been removed.

What might be on the platform could not be seen by those in the courtyard. All around it, from its railing to the floor, black cloth had been stretched.

Suddenly a sound like the whisper of far-off breaking surf spread among the multitude. It swelled quickly to a louder pitch of voices. People raised themselves on tiptoe and moved their heads, first this way and then that, to get a better view.

First, through the aperture where the window had been, came Colonel Hacker and his guard of soldiers. Next the slight figure of the King appeared, with Bishop Juxon by his side. The King's step was firm and steady.

Behind them came two men. They wore masks, false beards and wigs. A question fluttered from lip to lip among the crowd in the courtyard: "Who are they? Who are the men who agreed to do this?"

No one knew. No one has ever known beyond all doubt who they were.

The King surveyed the spectators calmly, then drew from his pocket a small piece of paper and glanced over the notes he had jotted on it. Other witnesses had now come through the aperture. In all there were fifteen of them on the platform. It was to them that the King began to speak.

At that moment there was a break in the lowering clouds that hovered over London. In the crowd the superstitious ones wondered what such an omen might mean.

The King spoke for some time. He said he was innocent

of the crime with which the Puritan leaders had charged him. Then he said, "I have forgiven all the world, and even those in particular that have been the chief cause of my death."

Death. Behind the black cloth around the platform was the scaffold on which the King was to die. Those looking down from the rooftops and the windows just outside the palace could see, behind the cloth, the little wooden block, the coffin of plain boards, and the glittering axe.

Now the King was speaking of the one great regret of his life. He had allowed his true and loyal friend, Thomas Wentworth, Earl of Strafford, to go to the scaffold. There had been reasons for it—good reasons—yet what he had done had been heavy on his conscience ever since.

"I will only say that an unjust sentence that I suffered to take effect is punished now by an unjust sentence upon me," he told those on the scaffold.

And finally: "I die a Christian according to the profession of the Church of England as I found it left me by my father."

The King then spoke to one of the disguised men—the executioner. "I shall say but a short prayer," he said. "When I hold out my hands, thus, strike."

The King then took the white cap from Juxon and put it on. He tucked his long curls under it to leave his neck bare. Then he disappeared from the view of those in the courtyard as he lay down with his head on the block. They saw only the flash of the axe as the executioner brought it down.

A spectator wrote later: "At the instant when the blow was given there was such a dismal, universal groan among the people as I never heard before and desire I may never hear again."

The executioner's assistant held the King's head high

for all to see. But he did not pronounce the words he had been told to say: "Behold the head of a traitor!" He did not dare, for if his voice had been recognized he would never have been safe from vengeance at the hands of the King's loyal friends.

King Charles I was dead. England had killed him. Rulers before him had been deposed from the throne or forced into exile. One who came after him would be ousted. But never before had an English king been executed—nor would another be afterwards.

What had caused England to rid itself of Charles I in this way? It was part of the struggle by the country's liberty-loving people for freedom, a struggle that had begun more than four centuries earlier.

2

The Beginnings
of Freedom

On June 15, 1215, in the pleasant meadow of Runnymede beside the River Thames above London, a historic meeting took place between King John of England and twenty-five nobles of the kingdom known as barons. Most unwillingly, though he really had no choice, King John signed the famous document called Magna Carta, the Great Charter.

It was the first stride toward freeing the English people from tyranny and persecution. Magna Carta, drawn up by the barons, promised many things. Most important, perhaps, was the clause which said that no freeman in England could be seized, imprisoned, deprived of his property, outlawed or exiled from the kingdom without a lawful trial before a jury of his equals. Another was that justice should not be denied or delayed to anyone. And there were many other sections designed to right wrongs which had been done in England.

Actually, the great mass of common people in England known as villeins received little immediate benefit from Magna Carta. Most of it applied only to freemen—owners of property. It was designed by the barons for their own selfish

17

purposes—to free themselves from wrongs the King had done them. The villeins, who were little more than slaves to the rich owners of the manors on which they lived, continued for years to be downtrodden, overtaxed and poverty-stricken.

Nor did King John keep the promises to which he had agreed. Yet Magna Carta lived on. In time all the people of England enjoyed the freedoms it stood for. Some of its provisions became cornerstones of English law and, later, of the Constitution of the United States.

People struggle to gain liberty, but they must continue to struggle to keep it. Not only John, but other rulers of England who followed him, neglected to obey Magna Carta's provisions. But time after time the people forced them to reaffirm the Great Charter and comply with its most important clauses. And gradually the people won other rights and freedoms.

One came when King Edward I saw that England would benefit by a better system of government. In 1295 he summoned a Great Council. It was composed of barons and high-ranking members of the clergy—both rich and powerful factions. Not only did it advise the King in governing the country, but it was also a kind of supreme court of the kingdom.

Other Great Councils, which were now becoming known as Parliaments, had been held for many years. What made the one in 1295 different was that for the first time it included representatives from the shires, or counties—knights, who were of lower rank than the barons, and officials known as burgesses. Some of the lower-ranking clergy also attended.

Thus, for the first time, the people of the middle class in England had their own representatives in Parliament. Edward I did this because he needed money to wage war against France. He could obtain it only by levying heavy taxes on the people. The King was wise enough to see that they would be less likely to revolt and refuse to pay if they agreed to these taxes through their representatives in Parliament.

He was scarcely prepared for what happened, however. In 1297 this Parliament of the people passed a decree stating that the King must levy no future taxes "except by the common consent of the whole kingdom." The King reluctantly accepted this. It was a victory for the rights of men. Nearly 500 years later the aroused people of America were to rebel against England to preserve this very principle of "no taxation without representation."

Nevertheless, Edward I had to have money, not only for the war but also to carry out improvements to bring greater prosperity to England. For many years the English kings had received certain revenues from fees, fines paid in court and the levies upon the rich estates of the barons and the property of the church. But this was no longer enough.

Parliament solved the difficulty by imposing customs duties upon various goods imported into England, as well as upon goods exported to foreign countries. Most of these duties were charged at so much a pound and were known as "poundage." On wines imported into England, however, they were charged on each of the big casks, called tuns, in which the wine was shipped. These duties were called "tunnage." Eventually the name "ton" for a weight of 2000 pounds was derived from the word "tun," and "tunnage" became "tonnage."

Edward I was granted this "tonnage" and "poundage" money for his entire life by the Parliament. So were the rulers who followed him until Charles I came to the throne. Then the question of whether he had a right to tonnage and poundage had a profound influence upon his fate.

The next advance in the achievement of rights and freedoms came in the reign of Edward III. During the sessions of Parliament from 1339 to 1341, the knights and burgesses separated from the barons and formed their own legislative body. It was the beginning of the House of Commons, representing the common people, and the House of Lords, composed of the high-ranking nobility or peers and clergy.

Gradually Parliament took even closer control of England's finances. Also during the reign of Edward III, it developed a means of ridding the country of corrupt ministers —the high officials of the government appointed by the King. To do so, it used the threat of its power to refuse him money. Until then, only he had been able to remove them. Now they could be impeached by the House of Commons and tried by the House of Lords for serious offences. They could be removed if they were found guilty, even executed for treason and other high crimes. Once again the power of the King had been weakened and that of the people made stronger.

Yet the peasants of England were still very poor; they lived in squalor and had almost no rights. They were cruelly taxed, and often they were unable to pay. In 1381 the government sent commissioners out into the villages to collect unpaid taxes. Led by a man named Wat Tyler, the peasants revolted, raised an army and marched on London.

There thousands of downtrodden journeymen and apprentices joined the 60,000 enraged peasants as they poured into the city. The rebels stormed the prisons, burning a notorious one, released the prisoners and captured the great fortress of the Tower of London.

But for the treachery of the King, Richard II, a boy only 14 years old, the rebels would have won their demands. During a conference between them and the King, Wat Tyler was murdered. Without his leadership the Peasants' Revolt collapsed. Richard then sent an army through the countryside which slaughtered many peasants and utterly crushed their resistance. Yet as a result of the revolt, taxes were reduced. In the years that followed, wages increased and gradually the villeins began to emerge from their slavery.

As the 15th century began, the power of Parliament became greater. Before then, persons who publicly criticized the actions of English kings were often imprisoned or otherwise severely punished. Now the members of Parliament demanded the right to speak freely when they disagreed with King Henry IV. In 1407 Henry proclaimed that the members might do so. This was a beginning of one of the liberties free people enjoy today—freedom of speech.

In the 15th century began the rule of the powerful Tudors, who reigned for just over a hundred years. During that time some of the gains the people of England had made toward greater freedom were temporarily lost.

Henry VII, the first of the Tudors, a cold, calculating, crafty man, was determined to weaken the power of the nobles. Through his influence the court known as the Star Chamber was created. It violated the great principle of Magna Carta that no freeman in England could be punished for a crime without a lawful trial before a jury of his equals. Persons summoned before it were tried without a jury. The lawful right of an accused person to hear the testimony of witnesses against him and to cross-examine them was ignored.

In one respect the Star Chamber was a good thing. English nobles often used their wealth and authority to bribe public officials to do their bidding and to force lower courts to decide cases in their favour. The Star Chamber stopped these fraudulent practices by meting out severe punishments to such offenders. But later the Stuart kings used the Star Chamber as a tyrannical means of striking at anyone who opposed them.

Three Tudor rulers kept Parliament strongly under their control. Henry VII made it do as he wished in most matters, but this was nothing compared to the way in which King Henry VIII and Queen Elizabeth I made themselves absolute rulers of England. One hears little of Parliament during either of their reigns.

Immensely strong-willed, Henry VIII governed almost as if there were no Parliament at all. He had his own ways of raising the money he needed, and while he did not try to force Parliament to obey him in other matters, he so dominated it that the members quite willingly went along with his wishes.

Under Henry VIII, England prospered and became stronger than it had ever been before. Nevertheless, he was a despot, though a benevolent one in most ways, and the rights and freedoms of the common people did not advance while he was King.

The next important ruler was Henry VIII's daughter Elizabeth. She was proud, arrogant and imperious, and at the same time wise, shrewd and clever. Like her father, she bent Parliament to her will without quarrelling with it. In her reign England became still stronger and more prosperous. The middle class gained greater power in Parliament, while that of the nobles became less. But otherwise the cause of the people's rights and freedoms advanced very little.

Elizabeth I left no children. Henry VIII's will decreed that after his own children the crown should go to the descendants of his sister Mary. But when Elizabeth died, the nobles of her Privy Council declared King James VI of Scotland as James I of England. Parliament seems to have become so used to obeying Elizabeth that it did not even dare oppose her councillors. James, the first of the Stuart kings, came to the throne.

He was an ungainly, coarse Scot who dressed like a tramp and whose manners were piggish. Yet he was a kindly, religious man who loved peace, and he proved a wise and astute ruler. One thing he insisted on, however, was his supremacy under the divine right of kings.

This doctrine held that a sovereign's right to rule came directly from God. Thus he did not have to have the people's approval of the way he governed them. He was responsible only to God, who had placed him on the throne. In other words: "The king can do no wrong."

It was against this very thing that Magna Carta stood, for its great foundation was that the king is not above the law. But James I believed that the king was above the law, Parliament and the people.

Parliament, so subservient to Henry VIII and Elizabeth I, now began to assert itself and oppose James I's despotic ideas. It fought fiercely with him all through his reign of 22 years. The King's principal opponent was the great lawyer, judge and member of Parliament, Sir Edward Coke. Once James became so enraged at Coke that he came at him "looking and speaking fiercely with bended fist," and the lawyer was so frightened that he fell to the floor. And while Parliament won a number of victories in this struggle, James never retreated an inch from his insistence upon supremacy.

The old Scot constantly drummed this principle of the divine right of kings into the head of his son, who became Charles I. He wrote to him: "The state of monarchy is the supremest thing on earth; for kings are not only God's lieutenants on earth and sit upon God's throne, but even by God himself they are called gods." James also wrote: "Majesty is made to be obeyed, not inquired into."

The divine right of kings was the chief cause of Charles I's downfall. But another powerful factor was religion.

Until Henry VIII came to the throne, England was a Catholic country. But a bitter quarrel arose between the King and the Church of Rome over his marriage. His wife, Catherine of Aragon, was a Spanish princess, daughter of Christopher Columbus's benefactors, King Ferdinand and Queen Isabella.

Catherine was a fine woman, but Henry was dissatisfied because all of their seven children had died soon after they were born except one, a girl. Since he wanted a son to succeed him, he decided to marry one of Catherine's ladies-in-waiting, Anne Boleyn. Because the Catholic Church did not permit its members to be divorced, Henry asked Pope Clement VII to annul his marriage to Catherine. The Holy Father refused.

In a fury, Henry VIII decided the Catholic religion must be abolished in England. At last, in 1534, Parliament yielded to his demands and passed the Act of Supremacy. It declared: "The king, our sovereign lord, his heirs and successors, kings of this realm, shall be taken, accepted, and reputed the only supreme head in earth of the Church of England. . . ."

This was the beginning of the Reformation, in which the Catholic Church was replaced by the Protestant one known as the Church of England, or the Episcopal Church. As a result, many faithful Catholics who refused to give up their religion were unmercifully persecuted.

After Henry VIII died, his daughter Mary eventually came to the throne. She was a devout Catholic who had not given up her faith. She succeeded in having the Act of Supremacy repealed. Now it was the Protestants who were persecuted under what were known as the Heresy Acts. More than 500 Protestants who refused to give up their religion were burned at the stake, and the Queen became known as Bloody Mary.

When Elizabeth I began her long reign after Mary died in 1558, the Church of Rome did not recognize her as Queen, since it considered Henry VIII's marriage to Anne Boleyn, her mother, as illegal. Elizabeth retaliated by prevailing upon Parliament to pass another Act of Supremacy.

With that, the Catholic faith as the official religion of England was finally ended. Yet the bitter struggle between Catholics and Protestants went on. Not only that, but the Church of England tried to abolish other forms of religion, especially those of the Puritans in England and the Presbyterians in Scotland.

This, too, had its effect on Charles I's fate. He was caught in the middle of the struggle over free men's right to worship as they pleased. He himself was a tolerant man in matters of religion. But in the hope of saving his throne, he yielded to the Church of England in some matters when he did not wish to.

The story of his journey over the road that led to his doom might well begin with an incident which occurred while Charles was still a boy.

3

A Journey to Spain

One bright spring morning a young man came whistling blithely over a path that led through the gardens of the ancient Palace of Greenwich, a short distance down the Thames from London. He was a tall, elegant, handsome fellow, dressed in the height of fashion. His short jacket, or doublet, of black and gold velvet, with a high lace ruff at the throat, fitted his trim figure perfectly above very full breeches of the same colour and material. Polished boots with wide-flared tops came nearly to his knees. On his head the plumes in a low-crowned, wide-brimmed hat waved jauntily.

Farther down the path, a boy of about fourteen peered out of his concealment in a clump of bushes. He was also elegantly dressed. His expression, always melancholy, was now as black as a thunderhead in the sky. Prince Charles, son of King James I, could not think of anyone he hated as much as George Villiers, the young man who was coming toward him.

"Steenie!" he muttered under his breath. He hissed the word again: *"Steenie!"*

That was what his father called his favourite, George Villiers, who was also a great pet of Charles's mother, Queen Anne. What made it worse was that Villiers was not only handsome, but stalwart; and his legs were well shaped and muscular.

Prince Charles looked down at his own spindly legs. The disease of rickets had so shrivelled them when he was a baby that for some years he had not been able to stand on them. Charles thought of what his older brother, Prince Henry, had once done.

The two boys had gone to discuss something with King James. The King was in his audience chamber, and when they reached it the door was closed. On a table in the anteroom outside lay a square cap of purple velvet.

"We will have to wait," said Henry. "That's the Archbishop of Canterbury's hat."

He picked it up and put it on his brother's head. "Ha!" he cried, "it's most becoming to you, Charles. When I am King you shall be my Archbishop of Canterbury. Then you will have a long cloak to cover your legs."

In a frenzy of anger, Charles tore off the cap, threw it to the floor and stamped on it. His brother and sister sometimes made thoughtless remarks, not only about his legs but about the stammer that also afflicted him. He was extremely sensitive about these things. Both his brother and his sister Elizabeth seemed so superior to him in every way that he fairly burned to have some small advantage over them. If it were only he instead of Henry who would one day be King.

There seemed small chance of that. Henry, the heir apparent to the throne, was strong and healthy. Moreover, no one really expected sickly Charles to live to manhood. But in 1612, when Henry was nineteen, he suddenly fell ill and died. Becoming the heir did not completely cure Charles's feeling of inferiority, however. That was why he was jealous of George Villiers. But he was resolved that when he became King he would be a real one like his father, tolerating no interference with his rule.

Now, on the garden path, George Villiers was only a few paces from Charles's hiding place. The prince stepped back and put his hand on the end of a spray pipe connected with the water supply of the palace. It was used by the royal gardeners to water the grass. Charles aimed it straight at the path. As George Villiers came abreast of him, he pulled out the plug.

The water rushed out in a deluge of spray. Villiers gave a startled cry, but before he could dodge out of the way his fine clothes were soaked.

He made a lunge toward Charles's hiding place. The prince had turned to run for the cover of some thick shrubbery, but Villiers was too quick for him. He seized Charles by the scruff of his neck.

The boy was frightened out of his wits. Villiers would surely tell his father, who could be very stern.

"Odd zooks!" Villiers cried, "I have you, my fine cully! Why, rot you, I'll—"

He stopped short as he saw who it was. Loosening his grasp on Charles, he fell to his knees. Water spurted from his sopping doublet and breeches.

"Your Royal Highness," he murmured, "I didn't know who—" Then he threw back his head and laughed uproariously. "Ho! ho! what a joke!"

"Y-y-you won't tell F-F-Father?" Charles stammered.

"Tell him!" cried Villiers. "Why, of course not, your Highness, though it's a pity he'll never know what a clever prankster his son is. I'll tell him I fell into the fish pond over there, trying to get a better look at a big carp in the water."

When Villiers had gone on, Charles pondered what had happened. His father's favourite had always tried to make himself agreeable, but the prince had scorned his friendly advances. Now he realized that Villiers was really a very decent fellow.

From then on, Charles was less distant toward him, and Villiers overlooked no chance to improve his standing with the heir to the throne. He desperately wanted fame and fortune, and he knew the day might not be far distant when Charles would be King.

George Villiers was probably the most charming young man who ever appeared at the English royal court. Handsome, accomplished, well-mannered, debonair and brilliant, he enchanted men and women alike. Now he began to enchant the boy who would be King.

Charles had set out to make himself strong and healthy. Each day he practiced running exercises. He rode horseback and mastered a great charger. In the hunts which were the favourite sport of English royalty and nobility, he became a crack shot.

Villiers praised all these accomplishments extravagantly. He treated Charles as a man, not a boy. At the same time, he deferred to him, making him feel the superiority of his royal rank. This was what Charles craved most of all.

Charles missed his dead brother. He missed his beloved sister Elizabeth too, for she had gone to Germany and married Frederick, the Elector, who ruled the province called the Palatinate. Then, in 1619, his mother, Queen Anne, died.

He was very lonely now, and needed friendship badly. He found it in George Villiers. Although George was eight years older, the two became inseparable companions. For Charles it was the one great friendship of his life—and a disastrous one.

Meanwhile, through the influence of Queen Anne, Villiers had been appointed a Gentleman of the King's Bedchamber at a high salary. A little later King James promoted him to be Master of the Horse. Soon afterward he was raised to the nobility, first as a viscount and then in succession to Earl and then Marquis of Buckingham. Thereafter George Villiers was always called Buckingham. And he was also appointed Lord High Admiral of the navy.

One morning early in 1623, Charles was summoned to his father's bedchamber. King James was not in bed, but with his scraggly beard and uncombed hair he looked as if he had just tumbled out of it after having slept in his royal robes of crimson velvet, trimmed with ermine, which were sadly rumpled. Buckingham was with him.

"Baby Charles," said the King, "it is time you were married."

"Yes, Father," replied the dutiful prince. What he thought of the name the King always called him no one knows, although he was now 22 years old.

"For some time I have been discussing it with my Privy Council, as well as with Steenie here," James went on. "We have decided that you are to marry Princess Maria, the Infanta of Spain."

Charles was not surprised. He knew very well that a bride for an heir apparent to the throne of England was usually chosen without so much as a thought of consulting the prince himself.

"You must know, Baby Charles, that we did not reach this decision without much discussion of its effect upon England," the King continued. "It was a question of whether your bride should be the Infanta of Spain or the younger sister of King Louis XIII of France, Henrietta Maria."

Charles nodded. He understood the planning and political intrigue which must have gone on. Spain and France were the principal threats to the kingdom among its possible enemies. Their dislike of England was due mainly to religion. Both were strongly Catholic countries. There had been great resentment in both when that religion was abolished in England under the Reformation. Charles's marriage to a princess from either country might help prevent a war and cement friendly relations.

Charles had a good idea why the Infanta, as a daughter of a Spanish king was called, had been chosen over Princess Henrietta of France. Spain was the richest nation in Europe and a formidable military power.

Moreover, Spain was an ally of powerful Austria. After Charles's sister Elizabeth married the Elector of the Palatinate, Austria had seized the little German kingdom, and Frederick and Elizabeth were forced to flee into exile. King James, Charles knew, was determined that the Palatinate should be returned to Frederick. Spain might induce Austria to give it back if the English prince married the Infanta.

Now King James continued: "If the negotiations for the marriage are successful, I shall probably send Steenie to Madrid as your proxy for the marriage."

This was no surprise, either. An envoy from one country was often sent to another to stand in place of a royal bridegroom at his wedding to a princess. Thus a prince and princess might be married some time before they ever saw each other. But Charles did wonder about the Infanta. What was she like? Was she pretty? He hoped so.

"Your Majesty," said Buckingham, "poor Charles ought at least to see the girl before he marries her. Why not send him to Madrid with your Majesty's dog Steenie?"

Buckingham was far from considering himself a dog, for he had been thoroughly spoiled by the King's favour

Nevertheless, he often referred to himself that way when he spoke to the King. It pleased James, and Buckingham knew it. As for his nickname of Steenie, the first time James had seen the handsome young man he thought of the Christian martyr Saint Stephen, who was described as "having the face of an angel." He always called Buckingham "Steenie," which is the Scottish equivalent of "Stevie."

At Buckingham's suggestion, a look of alarm crossed the King's face. "No!" he cried. "Consider the danger of such a long journey, Steenie. Remember that if anything should happen to Baby Charles, you would be blamed for it."

Buckingham, very cocksure of his standing with the King, smiled almost insolently. "Egad, your Majesty, you do fall into a mighty sweat over naught. Your dog will see that no harm befalls your son. Besides, if you refuse, he'll be monstrously pulled down over it, eh, Charles?"

Although the idea of such a jaunt would never have entered the prince's mind, he was tremendously intrigued now that Buckingham had suggested it. Taking the cue his friend had given him, he fell to his knees before the King.

"Father!" he implored, trying to make his voice tremble with emotion. "If you d-d-don't let me go, I s-s-swear I'll never marry!"

"I must talk to Cottington about this," muttered the King. He summoned a servant to fetch Charles's secretary.

"Cottington," said the King, "here are Baby Charles and Steenie, who have a great mind to go to Spain to fetch home the Infanta. What think you of the journey?"

Cottington, who dared not disagree with the King, saw his agitation and replied, "I cannot think well of it, Sire. Once the Spaniards get their hands on his Highness Prince Charles, they will make even stronger demands, especially about the Catholics here."

The King threw himself on his bed. He began to weep, and when he spoke he slobbered like some great lummox. "I am undone!" he wailed. "I shall lose my Baby Charles!"

The prince glanced at Buckingham. The marquis' thin, wide mustache and small, pointed beard gave him a devil-may-care expression. Now a contemptuous smile curled his lips.

"Who asked your opinion on matters of state, buffle-head?" he demanded of Cottington. "His Majesty only wanted your opinion as to the best route to Madrid."

The secretary cowered before his wrath. And so strong was Buckingham's influence upon the King that James finally wilted and gave his consent. Charles and his friend went off in high glee, making plans for the journey.

"If we are recognized, word of our coming will surely reach Madrid ahead of us and spoil the surprise," said Buckingham. "We'll wear big false beards and use false names."

And so, in their disguises, they set off on horseback February 10, 1623, for Madrid. With them went Cottington and two other young men who were their close friends.

Their adventures began when they crossed the Thames below London. The ferryman thought the two richly dressed young men were going to a lonely spot to fight a duel, forbidden by law in England. He told the magistrates at Gravesend, who sent a courier in pursuit, but the royal party easily outdistanced him.

Then they were mistaken for some fugitives who had escaped to England after murdering a high official in Holland. This time they were caught and taken before the mayor of Canterbury.

Buckingham yanked off his false beard. "How dare you detain the Lord High Admiral of England?" he said. "For good reasons I am travelling disguised with these members of my staff to inspect the royal fleet at Dover. Release us instantly!"

He was recognized, and all were freed with profuse apologies. They were off once more, chuckling over their success in hiding the prince's identity.

After crossing the English Channel, they reached Paris. It was an ancient gray walled town with many towers, turrets and grim, fortresslike buildings. Yet it was gay, with a special charm of its own which made it different from any other city. Buckingham, who had travelled extensively in Europe, delighted in showing Charles the sights.

Then he proposed a daring escapade. "We'll go to the Louvre," he said, "and see what the royal family is doing. But we must have better disguises. Some diplomat who's been at the court in London might recognize us."

To their beards they added curled periwigs. At the immense stone pile on the River Seine which was the French royal palace, they sneaked up to the doorway of the Grand Gallery. Peering in, they saw a score of elegantly dressed young ladies and a lad of about sixteen going through the steps of a dance.

"The Queen!" Buckingham whispered, pointing. "And that one is Madame, the King's sister. The boy is Monsieur, his brother. They're practicing for a masque to be held here."

Charles had eyes only for Queen Anne. He knew she was of the Spanish royal house and a sister of his intended bride, the Infanta. His heart raced, for she was very beautiful. If only Princess Maria were as lovely, he thought. He scarcely glanced at little Madame, the Princess Henrietta Maria. And she, with no idea that anyone was watching, did not see Charles. Later, when she learned of his visit to Paris, she said wistfully, "He need not have gone to Spain for a bride."

On March 7 the travellers reached Madrid, set in the

midst of a vast, barren plain, with snowcapped mountain summits edging it far to the north. The city was handsome, with broad avenues opening out from a central plaza and lined with the magnificent mansions of the rich, yet it was grim, with austere monasteries and convents everywhere to remind the visitor that Spain was Catholic to the core.

The party went to the house of the Earl of Bristol, the English ambassador to Spain. Bristol was stunned. He had been handling the marriage arrangements with all the tact of an experienced diplomat. This reckless adventure could not only upset these plans, but involve England in serious trouble with Spain. But he concealed his anxiety and welcomed the young men warmly.

It was no easy matter to arrange this marriage. The Pope in Rome would have to give his consent, and he was no friend of Protestant England. And the Infanta was so devout a Catholic that she had expressed horror at the thought of marrying a Protestant.

When King Philip and his chief minister, the Count of Olivares, heard that Charles was in Madrid, they reached the conclusion that he must have decided to become a Catholic. Then Olivares and Buckingham met to discuss the proposed marriage.

"The means are very easy," said the chief minister. "It is but the conversion of the prince, which we are certain was his intention when he decided upon his journey."

"You are mistaken, your Excellency," replied Buckingham. "His Royal Highness does not intend to become a Catholic."

"Then," said the chief minister, "we must send to Rome for a dispensation from the Pope to allow the marriage to take place." At the same time, he was determined that the prince must be converted, if possible.

Charles was impatient to meet his intended bride, but first there were endless formalities. Although King Philip himself came to Bristol's house and escorted the prince to apartments prepared for him in the gloomy, fortresslike Moorish palace of the Alcazar, he seemed no nearer to a meeting with Princess Maria.

Once he was established there, black-robed friars called on him and did their best to convert him to the Church of Rome. He listened politely, though he had not the slightest intention of changing his religion.

At last, on Easter Sunday, the King and a great train of Spanish nobles or grandees escorted Charles to the apartment where the Queen was seated with the Infanta by her side. When he saw Maria he was enchanted. She was a great beauty. Unlike most Spanish women, who were usually dark, the Infanta was fair-haired, with a complexion as soft and pink-and-white as apple blossoms.

As for Maria, she saw standing before her a slender, rather short young man who nevertheless had a noble bearing. He had a high forehead, very fine, silky, chestnut-brown hair, arched eyebrows, a thin mustache and lustrous eyes. For all his melancholy air, he was handsome and dignified.

Charles did remember to pay his respects to the Queen first. Then, as he turned to the Infanta, he forgot all the carefully rehearsed phrases he was supposed to say at this formal meeting and spoke from his heart. But to his dismay, Maria bridled and looked annoyed. She had already decided to dislike this Protestant suitor.

Then she spoke the words which had been written out for her—a few commonplace, meaningless phrases. Before Charles could open his mouth to reply, the ceremony was over and he was whisked back to his own apartments.

Now word arrived from the Pope that he would grant

the dispensation even if Charles did not become a Catholic. But he placed full responsibility upon King Philip to see that Catholics in England, Scotland and Ireland were no longer persecuted and would be allowed to worship freely in their chosen faith.

Olivares then called upon Charles. "I am commanded to tell you of his Majesty King Philip's decision," he said. "Your marriage to the Infanta will be allowed to take place in September, but she must remain here until March, when she will sail for England to join you."

Charles saw that the wily Spaniards proposed to hold Maria as a kind of hostage to make sure the Pope's demands were carried out. He knew that compliance with them would be all but impossible. In England there were too many powerful Protestant members of Parliament. Scotland was largely Presbyterian, and the Scots too were intolerant. And while Ireland was mostly Catholic, its religion had been ruthlessly suppressed by its English rulers.

"My father would never consent to such terms," Charles told Olivares. "If his Majesty insists upon them I shall call upon him tomorrow to take my leave."

But the prince was learning a thing or two about intrigue. Once he was married, he decided, he could get the Spaniards to yield on some of the demands and also let the Infanta go to England at once. Thus the Spanish King was astonished the next day when the prince appeared, for it was not to take his leave after all.

"I have resolved," said Charles, "to accept of my whole heart what has been proposed to me, both as to the articles touching religion and the security required." By "security" he meant the plan to keep the Infanta in Spain until spring.

King Philip threw his arms about Charles. "I embrace you as a brother," he said. Then he ordered the streets of

Madrid to be illuminated for four nights in celebration of the royal betrothal. A courier was sent to England with the glad tidings.

There, King James agreed to the terms. He could only hope that something might be worked out which the English Parliament would accept. And to his faithful "dog Steenie" he awarded the highest rank of English nobility, creating him the first Duke of Buckingham in gratitude for his success in arranging the marriage.

Charles still saw the Infanta only in the presence of the King or Queen or the highborn ladies who served her. He was deeply in love, or at least he thought he was. Why couldn't he be alone with his beloved?

Within the vast structure of the Alcazar were a number of walled courtyards and gardens. Passing along one of these walls one day with Buckingham, Charles wondered what was on the other side. He raised himself on tiptoe and peered over.

"Maria!" he whispered to his companion. "She's there in the garden—alone! Give me a leg up, Steenie."

Buckingham, always glad to oblige in a romantic adventure, boosted Charles over the wall. Hearing the thud as he landed, the Infanta looked up. Then she screamed and ran.

All well-born Spanish young ladies were protected against such visits of suitors by chaperons known as duennas. Before Charles could catch up with Maria, a veritable dragon of a duenna appeared. In no time she had the prince outside the wall again. There was a great scandal in the palace, but the sentimental Spaniards soon forgave the young man.

Now things began to go badly for Charles's romance. Some courtiers had been sent from England so that he might have a proper retinue for ceremonies and other formal occasions. They made all sorts of trouble. So did the newly created Duke of Buckingham. He seemed to have forgotten his suave manners, for he was insolent to the Spanish courtiers.

All attempts to convert Charles had failed, but one of his English courtiers yielded to persuasion and became a Catholic. His companions were outraged. Then he fell suddenly ill and was near death. A Jesuit priest appeared to give him the last rites of the Church of Rome, but the other courtiers barred the way, and one slapped his face.

The Alcazar was thrown into an uproar, and a bloody fight was barely averted. Charles immediately sent the offending courtier back to England, but King Philip demanded that all his Protestant attendants go home.

Offended and angered, Charles announced that he too would return home. Nevertheless, he was still determined to marry the Infanta. The wedding could be held by proxy. He took an oath that he would marry her and then returned by sea to England.

Once back in London, he was not so sure he wanted the Spanish princess as his wife. In Madrid his pride had goaded him to win this beauty who treated him so coldly. Now that she was far away, it was surprisingly easy to forget her.

Negotiations for the marriage continued, but the Spaniards now made new demands. While King James had hoped the marriage would aid in restoring the Palatinate to Elizabeth's husband, Frederick, he was not too disappointed. "I like not to marry my son with a portion of my daughter's tears," he said. The marriage never occurred, for trouble with Spain, which James had also hoped to prevent, flared up. Yielding to Parliament's wishes, he began to prepare for war with this ancient enemy.

The King decided he had better make France an ally if

possible. Negotiations for Charles's marriage to Louis XIII's sister were begun. At the French King's demand, a treaty was signed under which England promised to stop persecuting Catholic subjects. In return, France made an alliance with England, and the marriage was agreed upon.

Thus little Madame, the Princess Henrietta Maria of France, was betrothed to young Charles of England. The prince must have wished he had paid more attention that day in the Louvre in Paris, for he had not the slightest idea what she looked like. And Henrietta Maria, who had been so disappointed that Charles had gone on to Spain for his bride, had won the prize after all.

James ordered his "dog Steenie" to go to Paris as Charles's proxy for the wedding. But the King never saw his son's wife. He was not an aged man, only 59, but he was tired and in poor health. He fell ill of a fever, and on March 27, 1625, he died.

So it was that, three days after signing the marriage contract by which Henrietta would become his wife, Prince Charles became King Charles I of England.

4

The Struggle Begins

In the vast slums of London on June 18, 1625, carts were busy hauling away the bodies of those who had died in the streets overnight or had been thrown there. The plague had struck the city, as it had so often before and would again, no doubt.

Those who fell ill of this mysterious disease usually died soon and horribly, though a few survived. No one suspected that it was bred in the ramshackle, decaying rookeries where the poor lived in crowded squalor. No one blamed the piles of refuse and garbage thrown into the narrow alleys or the slime of the Fleet Ditch, a sort of open sewer which gave off an indescribably foul stench. Nor did anyone suspect that the brown rats scurrying in and out of all this filth carried the dread disease from one house to another.

Nevertheless, people who could not get out of London generally avoided contact with each other. That was why the crowd was smaller and much of the usual pomp was omitted when King Charles's coach made its way to Westminster that day to open his first Parliament. But those who did see him pass cheered enthusiastically.

The entire Parliament awaited the King in the chamber of the House of Lords. In the main section of the hall sat the hundred or so peers in their court robes. Beyond them, crowded into a small enclosure on the other side of a brass rail or bar, were the nearly five hundred members of the House of Commons. They had been summoned there from their own meeting place by the King's messenger, the Gentleman Usher of the House of Lords, who was called Black Rod because of the insignia of office he carried.

Amid respectful silence King Charles entered and walked toward the upper end of the hall. There he seated himself on a gilded, high-backed throne, elevated on a dais and covered by a canopy of crimson velvet supported by gilded columns.

In front of the throne and below it was the presiding officer of the House of Lords, the Lord Chancellor, often called the Woolsack because by ancient custom he sat on a square cushion stuffed with wool. There too sat his four colleagues of the Lords Commissioners, all in scarlet robes slashed with ermine.

A clerk rose and read the commission granting royal authority for the opening of this Parliament. Then the King rose to speak.

As he did so, all the members of Parliament took off their hats, as was customary. Charles too removed his crown and concealed it under his robe before replacing it on his head. This was not customary, but a gracious gesture of deference to this Parliament, with which he hoped to get along better than James I had with those during his reign.

Charles was nervous; he stammered when he began his address, and he apologized for his lack of ability as a speaker. Then he turned to the need for money to carry on the war against Spain. He reminded the members that they had urged the war.

"I beg you to remember," he said, "that this being my first action, and begun by your advice and entreaty, what a great dishonour it were to you and me that it should fail for lack of assistance from you."

As he continued, his eyes roved about the chamber, particularly the section occupied by the House of Commons. He knew many of its members already, for as a prince he had taken great interest in Parliament's activities and had himself sat in the House of Lords under his title of Duke of York.

There, for one, was John Pym. At first glance some might have thought him stupid—this massive, shambling, shaggy country squire whom the ladies of the royal court called "the Ox." But Charles knew better. Pym was not brilliant, but he had a bulldoglike tenacity, taking a grip on something he wanted done and hanging on until it was accomplished. Would he use these talents for or against the Crown?

There was Coke, James I's old opponent—tall, spare, long-faced, England's most distinguished man of the law. Magna Carta was his Bible. The old lawyer, who had served in Parliament during Elizabeth I's reign, had fought bitterly whenever James's use of his privileges—or the King's prerogative, as it was called—violated men's rights under the Great Charter. Coke would do so again if he thought the royal prerogative was being misused.

The King now urged Parliament to grant him the money quickly. With the plague raging in London, he did not want the members to risk their lives by staying in the city too long. Then he turned to another subject. "Lying tongues are at work," he said. "They say the King is less staunch a Protestant than his father. You must not listen to such falsehoods."

He was thinking of his lovely bride, Henrietta Maria. Only two days had elapsed since he had brought her to London. And this question of religion had been the only thing to cloud his joy at her arrival.

Charles's fears that she might be ugly had vanished when he met her at Dover. His fifteen-year-old Queen was a black-eyed, brown-haired beauty. She was charming too, and vivacious, nor was she as tiny as he had been led to believe. Surprised when he saw that she reached to his shoulder, Charles had stolen a glance to see if she was wearing high heels.

Henrietta noticed it. "Sire," she said, "I wear no high heels. I stand on my own feet." They were to prove prophetic words.

What had dismayed Charles, however, was that among Henrietta's retinue were a bishop and many priests of the Church of Rome. This was permitted under the marriage agreement, but the presence of so many Catholic clergy might cause trouble. James I's attempt to enforce the harsh Penal Laws against them had stirred the famous Gunpowder Plot, when Guy Fawkes, a Catholic, nearly succeeded in blowing up the very building where Charles was now facing his first Parliament. Protestant England had not forgotten it. That was why the King took pains to reassure Parliament that his marriage had not changed his devotion to the Church of England.

Again his gaze roved over the members of the Commons. Who else might oppose him? His eye fell upon Sir John Eliot. This member from Cornwall was a fiery orator who wanted the Penal Laws strictly enforced. John Hampden was there too, a rather shy, retiring man, but crafty, able to sway Parliament with the force of his arguments. He had opposed James I more than once.

Thomas Wentworth—haughty, testy, Protestant to the core—was a great landowner in Yorkshire, where he ruled his tenants like a little king. Yet he was a man with a passion for good government and a good man to have on one's side. Charles wondered. Could Wentworth be brought to the side of the Crown?

Having concluded his address, the King left the House of Lords, entered his coach and was driven back to Windsor Castle, up the Thames at a safe distance from the noxious, plague-ridden air of London. He was hopeful of loyalty and assistance from this Parliament. Indeed, for a short time there was an atmosphere of harmony. When the House of Commons held its first session, Sir Benjamin Rudyerd sounded a keynote of peace.

"I would remind you," he told the members, "that we now have a King bred in Parliaments. Let the Commons take such course now to sweeten all things between King and people, that they may never afterwards disagree."

Then, all at once, the roof of the House of Commons seemed to fall in, burying Charles's hopes under it. On the next day, Sir Robert Phelips rose to speak about the King's request for supply—the money to wage war on Spain. "We ought better to consider how we may supply our country's needs at home," he said. "I suggest that his Majesty's request be postponed."

Wentworth rose. "I move that a committee be appointed to draw a petition for that purpose."

Another member got up. "I urge that a committee be appointed to investigate the toleration of the Catholics, which has caused both their numbers and insolence to increase," he demanded.

It was decided that before anything else was done, the subject of religion should be taken up. A petition to the King was drawn up, asking him to restore the Penal Laws imme-diately. To this Charles returned a conciliatory answer. He would grant the petition, but he asked that Parliament trust him to do it in his own way.

As for the money the King needed, £140,000, no more than a pittance, was voted him. Meanwhile, the subject of tonnage and poundage came up. "The revenue of the Crown is being wasted," Phelips declared. "Before tonnage and poundage is granted his Majesty, we should impose some limitation on it."

A few days later the House of Commons passed a bill granting it to the King as usual, but only for one year, during which it would be investigated.

When Charles heard of it, he was stunned. For 200 years the rulers of England had been given this revenue for their entire reigns. True, the House of Lords declared that the Commons bill was an insult to the King and refused to approve it. But meanwhile, without the authority given him by the bill, Charles could collect none of the money.

As the days passed, the plague raged more and more fiercely in London. Many members of Parliament failed to appear at its sessions, preferring to remain in greater safety outside the city. At last Charles ordered Parliament trans-ferred to Oxford, a good fifty miles away.

He summoned Buckingham to discuss how to induce Parliament to give him more money. The duke also had much at stake, for he wanted to command the English forces in the war and gain even greater fame and prestige.

"I will call my friends in Parliament together to plan how it may be done, your Majesty," he said. "Eliot is one who can help us."

Eliot . . . ah! Charles knew that if influential Sir John would lead the fight, its chances of success would be excellent. And Eliot owed much to Buckingham. Through the duke's influence he had been appointed a vice-admiral.

It was not so easily achieved, however. Coke and Phelips joined in opposing the grant of more money and in attacking Buckingham. At Oxford, in the Great Hall of Christ Church, one of the colleges of the famous university, Coke rose and said that too much money had been wasted already.

"Where has it gone?" he demanded. "I will tell you where! In frauds of the King's officers and servants, in too many pensions and annuities to the King's friends, in mismanagement of the navy. The office of Lord Admiral is the place of greatest trust and experience. Young and unskilled men are not to be trusted with such great offices, and besides, multiplicity of offices held by one man is a great prejudice. Were I to go to sea, I would rather go with a man able to guide and manage a ship or fleet."

The Lord Admiral—Buckingham. Many who heard Coke felt he was right. It was true that the duke was no sea dog. He had little or no experience to qualify him for the highest post in England's navy. True, too, that he held many high positions because of King James's and now Charles's favour. Besides, he had obtained too much money from the royal purse for his relatives.

Phelips joined in attacking Buckingham. "It is not fit to repose the safety of the kingdom upon those whose abilities do not fit their positions!" he cried.

As for the additional grant of money—or subsidy as it was usually called—Charles himself pleaded for it before Parliament. He promised that if it would vote the subsidy it might remain in session until all its other grievances were settled.

Buckingham, too, appeared before Parliament. He said Spain would surely be defeated and the Palatinate restored to Elizabeth's husband, the Elector Frederick, for England would have strong allies in the war. Frederick's loss of the little kingdom was connected with the long struggle in Continental Europe known as the Thirty Years' War. Denmark and the Protestant region of northern Germany would support England against Catholic Austria, Spain and southern Germany, said Buckingham.

But the House of Commons was in no mood to comply. Coke fairly bellowed his defiance: "I will give his Majesty £1000 from my own purse rather than vote him another subsidy!"

And now the House of Commons was outraged when it heard a rumour that Buckingham had lent six warships of the English fleet to France. King Louis, it was said, planned to use them to put down a revolt by the Protestant Huguenots at the port of Rochelle in France. Worse, the story said that the cost of sending the vessels there and quelling the rebellion was to come out of the subsidy which had already been given Charles.

"Let us demand an answer from his Majesty whether this be true!" cried a member. This was done, and Charles sent Buckingham to reply. An insolent smile curled the duke's lips as he stood before the Commons.

"The French King will pay for the operation of the ships," he said. "As for their employment, it is not fit that kings give an account of their private counsels. You may judge of that by the events which follow."

This reproof did not make the House of Commons more kindly disposed toward the King and his request for more money. The extra subsidy was refused.

Charles was furious. He decided it was useless to hope that Parliament would change its mind. Very well. He would find other ways of raising the money. The war should be fought and the Palatinate restored to Frederick.

And since Parliament would vote him no more money, it should accomplish none of its own projects, either. One undisputed prerogative enjoyed by English kings through long-established custom was the right to order Parliament to assemble—and to prorogue it by commanding it to disperse and go home.

On August 12, 1625, Charles prorogued his first Parliament. The long struggle between the two which was to lead the King to the scaffold had begun.

5

The Beast Called
Stellionatus

"By the grace of God I will carry on the war if I risk my crown." So declared Charles after he had dismissed Parliament. "I shall send ships and an army on an expedition against Cadiz," he told Buckingham.

"Ha!" exclaimed the duke. "Then pray let me command it, your Majesty."

"No, Steenie," said the King, "I have other employment for you. I want you to go to Holland and negotiate with the Dutch for an alliance against Spain."

"Excellent, your Majesty," said Buckingham, who knew the Dutch were eager to fight the Spaniards. "But whence is to come the money for the expedition?"

"While you are in Holland, Steenie, I want you to arrange for a loan on the crown jewels from the merchants who deal in such matters. When the expedition returns from Spain there will be plenty of money to repay them. The ships will sail for Cadiz in time to capture it and then seize the Spanish treasure fleet when it arrives."

"The *Flota Plata*, of course!" cried the duke. "Their holds will be stuffed with gold, silver and jewels."

During the 16th and 17th centuries, Spanish *conquistadores* swarmed over South and Central America and Mexico. They subdued the Indians there and looted the rich mines of their treasure. Once a year the *Flota Plata,* or Silver Fleet of galleons, loaded cargoes of gems and precious metal and sailed for Spain. The fleet would be due at Cadiz in the autumn.

The King appointed Sir Edward Cecil to command the army against Cadiz. Buckingham went confidently off to Holland. He was successful in arranging the alliance, but in Amsterdam the shrewd moneylenders refused to pay as much as Charles had expected for the crown jewels.

Nevertheless, the King sent an army to Plymouth to embark aboard transports of the fleet. The vessels were not ready. Since there was no money to pay the soldiers, farmers in the region were forced to lodge the men, but they refused to feed them without compensation. The soldiers then took to stealing and looting the countryside. Hordes of them deserted. Cecil did little to train them for the assault on Cadiz.

Aboard the warships of the fleet, conditions were just as bad. The sailors were not paid either, and many also deserted. Most of what money there was to fit out the vessels for sea went into the pockets of corrupt naval officials and contractors. But at last the fleet sailed. It was sighted off the coast of Spain, and Cadiz was warned of its approach. Some old ships were sunk at the entrance to the port's inner harbour, blocking it.

When the English fleet arrived, it bombarded a fort guarding the approach to the city. Then Cecil landed his troops. They captured the fort and might have taken the town had they not discovered a large store of wine, which they drank to the last drop. The befuddled English troops had to be taken back aboard the transports.

The rigging and spars of the English ships were so

rotten that the cordage had broken continually during the voyage, and yards and booms snapped under the force of the wind. The food was scant and mouldy, the biscuit infested with weevils, and the men threatened with scurvy. Many sailors were already ill or too weak to work.

Reinforcements and a large supply of food had reached Cadiz, so it was prepared for a long siege. The English decided that it could not be captured. For all the world like the French king in the old rhyme who marched up the hill with 40,000 men and then marched down again, the expedition returned to England. It had been a miserable failure.

As for the Spanish treasure fleet, it had been warned to change its course and delay its arrival at Cadiz. On October 28 the English fleet sailed for home. On October 30 the galleons arrived at Cadiz. Their rich cargoes, with which Charles had expected to replenish his empty treasury, were safe.

On the Continent of Europe, things were no better for Charles's cherished hope of restoring the Palatinate to the Elector Frederick. The Danish troops which were to aid in the war had not marched. King Christian IV of Denmark was waiting for the money Charles had promised him to pay his soldiers. And the German army under Count Mansfeld, which was also to take part, had not moved either.

Charles decided he must summon a new Parliament and make another demand upon it for money. But first he saw to it that his chief enemies in the last one were silenced. Orders were sent out appointing Coke, Phelips, Wentworth and three other troublemakers as sheriffs in the shires in which they lived. They could neither disobey the royal command to serve nor sit in Parliament while they held these offices.

But this scheme was like trying to mend a gaping hole

Charles 1

Henrietta

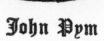

John Pym

Strafford

Archbishop Laud

in a dyke with a pailful of sand. Other members were ready
to take the places of the six men with demands that the King's
power be curbed.

Parliament was to meet on February 6, 1626. But first
Charles had to be crowned. The coronation was held on a
bright winter's day, February 2, in Westminster Abbey, with
all the pomp which down through the ages has made it one
of the most colourful and impressive rites in the world. It was
customary for a king of England to wear purple robes at the
ceremony, but Charles was all in white. He explained that
this was because he was like a bride being married to his
beloved subjects.

Westminster Abbey was jammed with the nobility of
England in their gorgeous coronation robes, members of the
House of Commons, ministers of state, judges of the high
courts, bishops and other high-ranking clergy, and officials
from all over England. Whatever space was left was filled
with as many of the common people as could squeeze inside.

Four times the Archbishop of Canterbury, in his cere-
monial robes as head of the Church of England, demanded
of those present, "Do you consent to the coronation of Charles
the First?" and each time came an answering shout: "God
save King Charles!" Then Charles took his oath of office,
was anointed with holy oil, invested with the ring, sceptre
and rod which were the insignia of his rule, crowned and at
last enthroned on the ancient chair first used by King Edward I in 1300 and enclosing the Stone of Scone.

Beside the throne stood an empty chair. It was for the
Queen, but because of her religion, the powerful Archbishop
of Canterbury had forbidden her attendance.

The King's marriage was not turning out happily. It
could have but for the religious bigotry of the Church of
England and most of the people toward the Catholics. It

caused endless bickering and quarrels between Charles and Henrietta.

Henrietta was devoted to the Church of Rome. She was outraged when the King agreed to enforce the Penal Laws against the Catholics. As for Charles, he was annoyed and made uneasy by the swarm of priests who surrounded his wife. Although they were protected against persecution by the marriage agreement, their presence caused much resentment in England.

Other things caused dissension between the two. Because Henrietta insisted that only the ladies-in-waiting she had brought from France might attend her, titled English ladies who had hoped to be part of the Queen's retinue were angered. And Henrietta hated Buckingham.

These were petty troubles, however, compared to those which beset the King as his second Parliament convened. He urged the members to grant him the money he wanted without delay, but they insisted on considering their grievances first. Foremost among them was Buckingham's responsibility for England's troubles at home, and also for the fiasco at Cadiz.

The leader in these demands was Sir John Eliot. Perhaps because he was jealous of Buckingham's high standing with the King and the many royal favours the duke had received, he turned suddenly against his benefactor. Their long friendship ended, and from then on Eliot bent all his energies toward destroying the duke.

"I beseech you, cast your eyes about!" Sir John cried in the House of Commons. "View the state we are in! Consider the loss we have received! View the wrecked and ruined honour of our nation—not by the sword, not by chance, but by those we trust."

He was speaking of Cadiz. While he did not mention

Buckingham by name, everyone in the House of Commons knew whom he meant.

Old Sir Edward Coke was not there to hear him, but his son Clem was, a tall, stalwart young man who had first been in Parliament in James I's reign. There his pugnacious speeches had earned him the name of "Fighting Clem." He supported Eliot's demand for an investigation of conditions in England. "Better to die by an enemy than to suffer at home!" he shouted.

The outraged King commanded the House of Commons to pass a bill allowing him tonnage and poundage within a week; otherwise, he warned, the money would be collected anyway. Then he summoned the House of Commons to Whitehall Palace and told the members they must take up the subsidy bill first. When it was passed they might have as much time as they wanted for their complaints. "To your just grievances I will always be ready to listen," he said.

As for the accusations against Buckingham, the duke had done everything he could for the welfare of the kingdom. "And yet you question him," the King continued. "Certain it is that I did command him to do what he hath done. I would not have the House to question my servants, much less one that be so near to me."

The King concluded by referring to what Clem Coke had said, and added, "Therefore I hope I shall find justice at your hands to punish such as shall offend in that way."

But nothing was done to punish Clem. Nor did the House of Commons pay immediate attention to the King's demands for money. It did propose to give him a small subsidy, but only after its grievances had been settled. And a committee was appointed to draw up charges against Buckingham.

Again Charles ordered the members of the Commons

to come to Whitehall. First, Sir Thomas Coventry, the Lord
Keeper, or presiding officer, of the House of Lords, spoke for
the King. He lectured them sternly because they had not
punished Clem Coke. By attacking Buckingham, he said,
they had attacked the honour of the King and his late father,
James I. And they must vote a larger subsidy for the war.

Then Charles spoke. Reminding them again that the
war had been undertaken by their advice, he said, "You
think I am so far engaged that there is no retreat, but I pray
you not to be deceived. I see that you especially aim at the
Duke of Buckingham. Remember that Parliaments are alto-
gether in my power for their calling, sitting and dissolution.
Therefore, as I find the fruits of them to be good or evil,
they are to continue or not to be."

Now that he had flung this direct challenge at the House
of Commons, it was accepted. The battle was on. The committee which had been appointed submitted thirteen charges
against Buckingham. On May 9 they were presented to the
entire House of Commons.

It was claimed that the duke had taken large sums of
the public money for his own use. Furthermore, he held too
many high posts, some of which he had bought. As Lord
High Admiral he had failed to have the navy stop piracy
against English merchant ships.

Other grievances included the ships lent to France and
the charge that the duke had sold jobs in the government.
Then John Pym rose and spoke of the honorary positions
Buckingham had secured for his needy relatives, who were
now being supported by the Crown. He went on to another
charge: that the duke had been given lands owned by the
Crown and had made a profit of over £160,000 by selling
some, while he had rented out others for over £3000 a year.

One other serious charge was that during James I's last

illness Buckingham had interfered with the royal doctors and administered a mysterious medicine of his own. Although no mention was made of it then, there were those who whispered that the duke had poisoned him. Indeed, a little later, Sir Dudley Digges, one of the King's opponents, hinted not only that Buckingham had murdered the old King but that Charles himself had also had a hand in it.

Finally, Sir John Eliot summed up the charges. "What vast treasures he has got!" he cried. "What infinite sums of money and what mass of lands! If you please to calculate, you will find it all amounting to little less than the whole of the subsidies the King hath had during that time. No wonder the King now is in want, this man abounding so."

Of the duke's character, Eliot said, "I can express it no better than by the beast called by the ancients *stellionatus* [a Latin word meaning a lizard], a beast so blurred, so spotted, so full of foul lines that they knew not what to make of it."

Eliot's tactless outburst may have inflamed some of the hotheaded members like himself, but a cooler head was needed to present a legal case against Buckingham. Behind the scenes, John Pym was preparing just such a case.

When Pym made a speech, it was far more moderate than Eliot's. But he had one thing to say that the House of Commons would remember: "If you look upon the time past, never so much came into any one private man's hands out of the public purse." Buckingham would find that hard to disprove.

The King was seething against Eliot and Digges. This time he would not plead with the House of Commons to punish the two offenders. He would do so himself.

Meanwhile, the Commons impeached Buckingham by a vote of 225 to 106. Now he had to be tried by the House of Lords, his equals. One of the members of Commons was sent to the Lords to ask that the duke be imprisoned until his trial was over. This, however, the peers would not do.

While the House of Commons awaited its emissary's return, Eliot and Digges were summoned outside the chamber. A little later someone noticed that they had not come back to their seats. An uproar arose when the word flew from member to member: "Eliot and Digges have been arrested for treason on a royal warrant! They are already on their way to the Tower of London!"

John Pym tried in vain to quiet the tumult. At last the members left the chamber, muttering threats of retaliation against the King's high-handed action.

The next morning, as the Commons assembled, the Speaker rose as usual to declare it in session. But he could not make himself heard. From all directions came shouts of: "Sit down! No business till we are righted in our liberties!"

The House of Commons seemed determined to sit no more until the two members were released from their imprisonment in London's vast medieval fortress, the Tower. Even the House of Lords, more kindly disposed toward Charles, had its objectors. A protest was signed by thirty-six of the peers, declaring that Digges had said nothing treasonable.

The King was finally forced to release both men, but the House of Commons was still vindictive. On May 24 it passed a resolution declaring that tonnage and poundage were illegal unless they were granted by Parliament.

When Buckingham's trial began, the least worried over the outcome was the duke himself. He appeared before the House of Lords in his own defence, as elegantly dressed and debonair as ever. He treated the charges with contempt as he replied to each one.

True, he said, he had received many honours from the King, but he had not sought them. He added, "I would readily lay down at his royal feet not only my places and offices, but my whole fortunes and my life to do him service."

He had plausible answers for everything. Yes, he had bought a position or two, but always so that he could better serve the kingdom. He shrugged as he spoke of the profitable posts held by his relatives. King James had honoured them of his own free will. It was really not worth discussing.

As for the claim that huge sums of public money had gone into his pockets, the accounts of the treasury would prove it false. And the navy, contrary to the charge against its Lord High Admiral, kept a powerful fleet scouring the seas for pirates. The charge of interfering with the doctors when James I lay on his deathbed was of course ridiculous. And in this last denial, at least, he was undoubtedly right.

Meanwhile, the King sent a message to the House of Commons demanding that a subsidy bill be passed within a week. Instead, the Commons voted to go ahead with drawing up a message to the King known as a remonstrance, demanding that Buckingham be removed from the positions he held.

Charles knew what a powerful weapon the Commons held. If he refused to dismiss the duke, he would get no subsidy. Meanwhile, Buckingham might be convicted by the House of Lords, removed from his posts anyway, and perhaps sent to prison.

To prevent this, the King used his most powerful weapon, informing Parliament that it would be dissolved June 15. A delegation from the House of Lords came to Whitehall. "We humbly pray that your Majesty will grant us two more days," their spokesman pleaded.

"Not a minute," snapped Charles. And as his second Parliament was dissolved, he was determined that he would do without it and somehow get the money he needed.

6

"A Sea of Troubles"

Now that Charles was rid of his balky Parliament, money was still his greatest problem. He had several plans for raising it. First he demanded a loan of £100,000 from the City of London, offering the crown jewels as security. It was refused.

Although Parliament had given the King no authority to collect tonnage and poundage, he was determined to have it. He called in the Crown lawyers. "Pray give me your opinion upon the King's right to collect tonnage and poundage," he told them.

The learned attorneys, who depended upon the King's favour for their positions, solemnly declared, "The collection of tonnage and poundage by the sovereign has been well established for many years as a royal prerogative. It is legal to collect it without a grant of authority from Parliament, your Majesty."

Charles then ordered the customs duties collected at all English ports to be handed over to him. But he was going to need much more money to wage the war on Spain. He decided to demand "free gifts" from his subjects. It was actually a sort of income tax, with the amount based on a person's ability to pay.

It could be collected, Charles thought, by the justices of the peace in the various shires or counties of the kingdom. The difficulty was that a number of the King's enemies in Parliament were justices of the peace as well. Charles took care of that by dismissing them and appointing others in their places.

Meanwhile, he was anxious to have Buckingham cleared of the charges against him. Why not have him tried before the Star Chamber? Since no juries sat on such cases and the judges were appointed by the King, there was no trouble in establishing the duke's innocence. The judges dutifully declared Buckingham not guilty, but his troubles were far from over.

The King was worried about his plan for a free gift, since it violated free men's liberties by being imposed without the consent of the people through their representatives in Parliament. He decided to try it out first in Westminster. Westminster was not then part of London, but a separate city surrounding the buildings in which Parliament and the high courts of the kingdom sat. All who were liable for the free gift were summoned to vast Westminster Hall.

The crowd was openly rebellious. From all sides came shouted demands for "A Parliament! A Parliament!" Only thirty persons agreed to pay, all of whom held positions from which the King could remove them if he chose.

Nevertheless, he went ahead with the plan. Attempts to collect the free gift were then made throughout England. Gifts were received from a few nobles who depended heavily upon the King's favour, but the plan was a dismal failure. Charles was going to have to find some other way to get the money.

In August he sold 70,000 ounces of the royal plate—dishes and other household articles of silver and gold. More was sold in September. But this could only relieve his need temporarily.

Other troubles beset the King. The quarrels with Henrietta had become more frequent. He had fallen in love with her at first sight, but now both were unhappy.

Most of the disagreements were over the Queen's French attendants. They grumbled, complained and treated everything that was English with rudeness and contempt. There was jealousy and hatred between Henrietta's ladies-in-waiting and the noble ladies of the English court.

At last Charles told the Queen her attendants were to return to France. There was a stormy scene, until the King yielded to her tearful entreaties and allowed her to keep a few of her favourites. The others were defiant and refused to go. When they were forced to, they left a veritable mountain of unpaid debts in London and stole some of Henrietta's jewels and her finest gowns.

In France, King Louis was indignant over Charles's action, but he wanted to save his sister's marriage if possible. He sent François de Bassompierre to London to see what could be done. Bassompierre was the very man for such a mission. A great favourite of the famous Henry IV as well as of his son Louis, he was a statesman, clever, bold, suave, skilled in intrigue. Best of all, ladies adored him.

Henrietta fell completely under Bassompierre's spell. She did not argue when he told her bluntly that she was more to blame for the quarrels than Charles. As for the King, when Bassompierre suggested that a somewhat smaller but more carefully chosen retinue be sent from France, he agreed. And the Queen accepted a proposal that some of her ladies-in-waiting should be English.

Charles fell in love with Henrietta all over again. To his intimates he said, "The only dispute between us is over which loves the other more." And for the rest of his life he was a loving and considerate husband.

Charles's troubles over the war were not so easily solved. From the Continent came ominous news. Count Mansfeld, commander of England's German allies, had been routed by the Austrian army and was in headlong retreat. The army of King Christian IV had also been defeated and driven back to Denmark.

At Portsmouth, where the English fleet was based, the sailors were unpaid and on the verge of mutiny. One day in August when Buckingham was returning from the Admiralty to his home in Essex, outside London, his coach was stopped. The duke peered out of the window and saw a mob of 200 angry sailors milling about the vehicle. They had made their way from Portsmouth to London.

Buckingham heard shouts: "Pay us! We want our pay!"

They were in an ugly mood. Some of the sailors held the horses' bridles, while others menaced the duke with upraised fists and muttered threats of violence.

"Let go of the horses so my coachman can turn about," Buckingham ordered. "Come to the Admiralty later in the day and you shall be paid, my buckos."

But he knew there was no money at the Admiralty or anywhere else to pay the men. When the coach headed back toward Whitehall Palace, the driver whipped the horses to full speed and outdistanced the mob. Instead of going to the Admiralty, Buckingham was driven to the palace landing on the Thames. There he boarded a boat and escaped down the river to his home.

The King was nearly at his wits' end for a source of more money. He called a meeting of his Privy Council.

"Your predecessors have sometimes used a forced loan successfully, your Majesty," one suggested.

"The very thing," Charles agreed. "My subjects will be more willing to pay, knowing the money will be returned to them later. And we will use drastic measures to punish any who refuse."

It was true that forced loans had been used before, but never for such a large amount as Charles proposed to raise. Nevertheless, the plan was tried out in Middlesex County. Most of the people paid, fearing punishment if they refused. The elated King decided to extend the forced loans throughout the kingdom. Commissioners were appointed to collect the money.

There was immediate trouble. A number of the commissioners refused to serve. In several counties many people refused to pay. So did a dozen or more high-ranking peers. These nobles were summoned before the Privy Council to answer for their disobedience.

Persons who were neither rich nor titled were dealt with more harshly. Many who refused were sent to Portsmouth to serve in the fleet, a terrible punishment, since enlisted men in the navy were at the mercy of hard-fisted officers and vicious captains. Others were sent to Germany to face the enemy's bullets there.

During this time, England's relations with France were becoming worse. The French suspected that English ships were carrying contraband goods which were smuggled into France without payment of customs duties. French warships began stopping and searching English merchantmen. At last four of them were seized by the French off the port of Rochelle.

Then, for no apparent reason, the French governor of Bordeaux seized two hundred English and Scottish ships at that port. They were not carrying contraband, since they had loaded wine cargoes there. Charles retaliated by directing that all French ships and their cargoes in English waters be seized.

France struck back by making an alliance with Spain. Now Charles faced a war with both. And the forced loan gave no promise of providing enough money to fight the war the King already had on his hands, let alone a new adversary.

Two of Charles's opponents, Sir John Eliot and Thomas Wentworth, had refused to pay the loan. The King sent Eliot to prison, though he dealt more leniently with Wentworth, ordering him confined to a private house in the county of Kent, where he could not influence the people of his far-away home in Yorkshire against the loan.

By late in the autumn, however, most people had been frightened into paying by the punishments others had suffered. The forced loan had brought in £240,000, nearly what had been hoped for.

Even this was not enough. The King sold some of the Crown lands for £143,000, and in December the City of London agreed to lend him £120,000. Yet £200,000 a year was needed just to pay the men of the army and navy, not to mention all the other expenses of waging the war.

The country would have got along very well but for the war. It was unpopular with almost everyone. Even the members of the King's Privy Council urged him to seek peace.

He discussed it with Buckingham. "What think you of negotiating with the French, Steenie?"

"Let all men beware of dealing with Frenchmen," replied the duke. "They are thoroughly false."

"I do not favour it, either," said the King, "but I must somehow raise more money to fight them."

"Summon a Parliament, your Majesty."

"They would try you under your impeachment, Steenie."

Buckingham fell to his knees. "If they find me worthy of death, let them not spare me!"

But the King would not risk his friend's life. Since he could not fight a full-scale war against France, he decided on a smaller offensive, an expedition against Rochelle. Giving aid to its Huguenot population, which was in revolt against Louis XIII, would be popular in Protestant England.

"We will send a fleet and troops to Rochelle," Charles told the duke. "You will be in command, Steenie."

As cocky as ever, Buckingham had not the slightest idea that the expedition could fail when his fleet of 100 vessels carrying 6000 infantry and 100 cavalry sailed in June, 1627. The ships anchored off the island of Rhé, which commands the entrance to the harbour of Rochelle. The King had told Buckingham to ask the inhabitants if they wanted help. Perhaps they feared the French King's vengeance, for their answer was hesitant and doubtful.

The duke decided to capture Rhé anyway. From it, English privateers could sally out to capture valuable prizes when French ships went into or out of Rochelle's harbour. And a profitable salt works on the island would produce revenue for the all but empty royal treasury.

Then an unbelievable series of blunders took place. They were due largely to inefficiency and negligence. Buckingham, an able commander, showed great courage and bravery himself, but the troops were poorly trained and disciplined, disgruntled over the wretched food and bad living conditions aboard the transports. The officers were not much better.

When the soldiers were landed, many tried to flee back to the boats. Buckingham strode among them, cursing, threatening and delivering lusty blows with a cudgel. Just then

200 French cavalry from the fort at the town of St. Martin's charged and drove the men into the sea, where some were drowned. But at last the enemy horsemen were repulsed.

The invaders began digging trenches and throwing up earthworks, on which cannon brought ashore were mounted. Although the French fort was well defended by 1200 infantry and the 200 cavalry, it could not hold out long unless food reached it. And the English warships were guarding against that.

Buckingham did not want to wait, however. With more men he could assault the fort and capture it. He dispatched a fast vessel to England with an appeal for reinforcements. The King sent back word that they would soon be on the way.

Then an emissary from the fort brought an offer of surrender. The duke was jubilant. He prepared to discuss the terms with the fort's commander. Then a second flag of truce came with a request for a delay until the next morning. Buckingham made his first blunder by granting it.

The second blunder came that night, when twenty-nine boats carrying food and other supplies for the fort sneaked through the very middle of the English fleet. No one knows why those aboard were so negligent as not to see them.

Now the French were ready for a long siege. Buckingham waited in vain for the promised reinforcements, whose departure from England had been delayed by fierce storms in the English Channel.

So many of the soldiers had fallen ill in the cold, damp trenches that it was decided to abandon the siege. Then the inhabitants of Rochelle changed their minds and begged the English to stay. The orders to sail for home were countermanded.

Now came the third blunder. A small fort on the island,

called La Prée, could easily have been taken, but not even the approach to it from the mainland was guarded. A large French army had arrived at Rochelle; little by little, soldiers were sneaked over to La Prée until there were nearly 6000 men in the two forts.

Buckingham decided to storm the St. Martin's fort. The English troops were driven off and many were slaughtered. Then the 6000 French attacked the English fortifications.

A fourth and last blunder had been made. Buckingham had prepared for the withdrawal of his army to safety if a retreat became necessary. A bridge had been built from Rhé to the smaller island of Loix, close by. But this means of escape had not been fortified.

The French force swarmed over the English trenches, and Buckingham's army was forced to retire. The duke stationed some cavalry at the bridge to cover the infantry's retreat. The French charged these unprotected horsemen and drove them into the middle of the English foot regiments, throwing them into confusion. Then other French troops attacked from the rear.

It was a massacre. About 3000 English soldiers were butchered or captured. Yet when the Rochelle expedition limped back to England, Charles welcomed Buckingham affectionately. He laid the defeat to the failure of the reinforcements to arrive.

But the rest of England blamed the duke. From then on he was probably the most hated man in the kingdom. And certainly, as the commander of the ill-fated expedition, the responsibility could fall only upon him.

The King, too, was disliked as a result of the disaster. He decided he had better make some sort of gesture to restore his popularity, and he ordered all those who had been punished for refusing the forced loan to be released. But it did little to make the people feel more kindly toward him.

Now the problem of money was worse than ever. Toward the end of January, 1628, the Privy Council met every day to discuss it with the King. At last some of the most influential noblemen in the kingdom came to him.

"You must summon another Parliament, your Majesty," they advised him. "A subsidy is the only way of avoiding financial ruin."

The King's jaw set. "I will not have Steenie tried."

"We will give you our personal guarantee that our influence will be strong enough to prevent it," was the reply.

The King thought it over for a time. At last, late on the night of January 30, he reluctantly issued writs calling a new Parliament to convene.

7

Petition of Right

When the 1628 Parliament convened on March 17, neither Charles nor its members were in a conciliatory mood. In the elections of members to the House of Commons, candidates who had opposed the forced loan had won their seats easily. They were not well disposed toward the King. And this time Charles had not been able to foil his principal enemies by appointing them as sheriffs. These selections had been made, as was customary, in November, before the elections. Sir Edward Coke, Phelips, Wentworth and the rest were back.

The King glowered from his throne as he addressed the two houses on the opening day. "I think there is none here but knows what common danger is the cause of this Parliament, and that supply is the chief aim of it," he said. "If some—which God forbid—should not do your duties in contributing what this state at this time needs, I must use those other means which God hath put into my hands. Take this not as a threatening, for I scorn to threaten any but my equals, but as an admonition from me who hath care for your preservation and prosperity."

But it was a threat to dissolve this Parliament too if it did not do his bidding. Nor was Charles's insinuation that the members were not his equals a tactful remark. Yet within eight days there was some evidence that Parliament might cooperate with the King, provided he would do the same with them.

Again, Sir Benjamin Rudyerd was the peacemaker. He spoke in favour of granting the King a large subsidy. But he also appealed to him to settle the grievances of Parliament.

"This is the crisis of Parliaments!" he cried. "We shall know by this one if Parliaments live or die. If the King draw one way and the Parliament the other, we must all sink." And he said Parliament ought to vote a large grant of money and then ask the King to remedy all the grievances.

But Phelips wanted more positive action on them. He said that merely debating the subject reminded him of the slaves of ancient Rome, who were allowed to speak freely of their oppressions on one day of the year, but on the next day they were back in their bondage, no better off then before.

"Now we have, as those slaves had, a day of liberty of speech," he continued, "but shall not, I trust, be herein slaves, for we are free; we are not bondsmen, but subjects."

Wentworth made a speech in which he said the King had gone too far in the use of his prerogative. There must be no more forced loans, imprisonment or forced military and naval service for those who refused to pay illegal taxes, he said, and no more lodging of soldiers upon people without their consent.

But he urged a reconciliation with the King. "The business of Parliament is to produce union between the King and his people," he said. "Both have been injured by past evils and both seek a remedy for those evils." And he recommended that the King be granted all the money he needed.

Sir Edward Coke was more disturbed over the forced loan than anything else. Let the money be granted, he said, but put into the bill a statement that forced loans were illegal.

Nevertheless, the King could hardly believe it when the secretary of the House of Commons called upon him to report that the money he had asked had been voted him.

"By how many votes was the bill passed?" Charles asked.

"By only one, your Majesty."

The King's face darkened, but it grew brighter when the secretary added, "It was voted by *one voice,* and by general consent."

"I liked Parliaments at first," said the King with one of his rare smiles, "but I grew to distaste them. Now I feel as I did at first."

But he soon found that Parliament, having done its part in yielding, expected him to do the same. It began, oddly enough, in the House of Lords, whose peers were, on the whole, more friendly to the Crown than the House of Commons. The Lords drew up a list of remedies for Parliament's grievances, those which had so often been debated in the Commons. It urged that the King, as several of his predecessors had been made to do, should declare Magna Carta still in force.

When the King had read it, he sent a message to Parliament, promising he would reaffirm Magna Carta, but there must be nothing new added to it. As for the grievances, they fell under his royal prerogative. His subjects, he promised, should have no cause to complain of any wrongs or oppressions of their just rights and liberties. But they must rely on his royal word for that.

Sir Edward Coke was not prepared to rely on it. "Let us put up a Petition of Right," he proposed. "Not that I distrust the King, but I cannot take his trust but in a parliamentary way." He meant that the King must approve the remedies for the grievances in writing; otherwise he might declare later that some were not wrongs or oppressions.

In his speech before the House of Commons concerning grievances, Wentworth had laid the foundation for the great document known as the Petition of Right. Coke, with his razor-sharp legal mind and wide knowledge of English law, particularly Magna Carta, was chiefly responsible for the form in which it was drawn up. It had four main clauses:

1. "No man shall hereafter be compelled to make or yield any gift, loan, benevolence, tax or such like charge without common consent by Act of Parliament." Thus taxation by the King's prerogative was to cease.

2. "No man shall be compelled to answer . . . or be confined or otherwise molested or disquieted. . . . No freeman in any such manner as before mentioned shall be impressed or detained." Thus the King could no longer by his own authority put people in prison, confine them in their houses or those of other persons or force them into military service.

3. Compulsory billeting of troops with private citizens was to cease. In the future, soldiers could only be lodged in people's houses if they agreed to have them.

4. Martial law, except in time of war, should cease. Parliament recognized that such rule of the kingdom by military force, with the regular laws suspended, might be necessary in wartime. But its use in peacetime under the sole authority of the King was giving him too much power.

Under the clause concerning taxation the King's greatest power was taken away from him. It reaffirmed the right to which Edward I had been made to agree in 1297. In the future, only Parliament, whose House of Commons was composed of the people's representatives, was to levy taxes.

The clause concerning imprisonment restated an important one in Magna Carta: "No free man shall be taken or imprisoned . . . or exiled or in any way destroyed . . . except by the lawful judgment of his peers and by the law of the land." Other rulers before Charles I had violated this provision. But now Parliament decided to end a practice which Charles considered his royal prerogative.

When the Constitution of the United States was drawn up in 1786, the wise leaders who framed it included these two principles of the Petition of Right. Article I provides that only the people's representatives in Congress may levy federal taxes. Among the first ten amendments which form what is known as the Bill of Rights is one covering the principle expressed in the Petition of Right's clause on imprisonment, forbidding "cruel and unusual punishments." The Bill of Rights also prohibits billeting of soldiers with private citizens without their permisson.

Each of the states has a Bill of Rights in its constitution which protects the same liberties of its citizens.

Thus all Americans owe a debt of gratitude to Sir Edward Coke, Thomas Wentworth and the other Englishmen who fought for the people's liberties and against the wrongful use of power by English rulers.

There was much debate in Parliament over the Petition of Right. The House of Lords proposed that the King should still retain "that sovereign power [his prerogative] wherein your Majesty is trusted for the protection, safety and happiness of your people."

In the House of Commons, Sir Edward Coke leaped up with a strong objection: "I know the prerogative is a part of the law, but sovereign power is not a parliamentary word. In my opinion it weakens Magna Carta and all our statutes, for they are absolute, without any saving of sovereign power. Take heed what we yield unto. Magna Carta is such a fellow that he will have no sovereignty."

The House of Commons took heed, and the Petition of Right was passed without the addition. Now the King had to approve it.

Charles dared not refuse his assent, especially after Parliament had voted the subsidy. He was going to need more grants of money later, too.

On June 7, 1628, the King appeared before Parliament. With a shrug he signified approval of the Petition of Right by a phrase in French: *"Soit drot comme il est desiré."* ("Since it is so desired, let justice be done.") He did not for a moment mean that he intended to obey it when his prerogative was concerned. He showed it in his next words:

"This I am sure . . . is no more than I granted you in my first answer [when he promised that his subjects should enjoy their just rights and liberties], for the meaning of that was to confirm all your liberties, knowing . . . that you neither mean to hurt my prerogative *nor can.* You see how ready I have shown myself to satisfy your demands, so that I have done my part. Wherefore, if this Parliament have not a happy conclusion, the sin is yours. I am free of it."

They applauded him enthusiastically. There was great rejoicing among the people too when they heard that the Petition of Right was approved. That night bonfires blazed in the streets all over the vast City of London.

But Charles had once again flung a challenge at Parliament. This was the lesson he had learned at old King James's knees. His father had fought with Parliament too and never yielded an inch of his prerogative. Charles was just as doggedly resolved not to yield.

The challenge was not ignored. Four days later, the House of Commons passed another remonstrance. It charged that Buckingham alone was responsible for all of England's troubles and demanded that the King remove him from the posts he held so that he could no longer dominate the kingdom's future.

"Let me go before Parliament and answer them, your Majesty!" the duke demanded.

"No, Steenie," replied the King. "I will make certain that they will proceed no farther in this matter."

He refused the demand and notified Parliament it would be dissolved on June 26. The House of Commons retaliated by sending the King another remonstrance. In spite of Parliament's objections, Charles had been collecting tonnage and poundage. The remonstrance demanded that he cease doing so. But before it could be passed, June 26 came and Parliament was prorogued.

Charles did not completely dissolve it, however. It would meet in a second session in January, 1629. But once again, for the time being, at least, the King's dearest friend was protected against his enemies in Parliament.

8

Buckingham

One fine spring evening in that June of 1628, a certain Dr.
Lambe was making his way through Cheapside. He had attended a performance at the Fortune Theatre in nearby
Cripplegate. Now he was headed toward one of the scores of
taverns in Cheapside for some supper.

The shops were still open along that wide thoroughfare
which cut through the heart of what was then and is now
known as the City, for it once had been all there was of
London, walled in by its Roman conquerors in the 2nd
century. Quaint signs over the doorways indicated the com-
modities in which the shops dealt—the Golden Leg of a hosier,
the Boot of a shoemaker, the Hand and Glove of a glover,
and many others.

Cheapside was thronged with people meandering along
in hopes of finding a rare bargain in a piece of fine linen, a
hat for milady or a bit of jewellery wrought by the art of one
of the many goldsmiths there. Strolling peddlers hawked their
wares, and street singers chanted the latest popular ballads.

The words of one song caught Dr. Lambe's ear, for it concerned him and the Duke of Buckingham.

Everyone in London was familiar with the scurrilous ballads about the hated duke. Dr. Lambe had already heard the one about himself. He was not a real doctor, but a quack who dosed his patients with worthless remedies, all guaranteed to cure anything from a headache to the most fatal diseases. He was also an astrologer, reading miraculous fortunes for all in the stars. And he dealt in love potions. Although Buckingham needed no such concoctions to charm ladies, he was reputed to be one of Dr. Lambe's best customers.

Lambe, wrapped in thoughts of the play he had seen, paid little attention to those about him until a chorus of hoots and catcalls made him look up. He was surrounded by half a dozen apprentices.

One saw the apprentices of London everywhere, wearing the aprons identifying the trade they were learning—leather for a blacksmith, white for a grocer, blue for a wine vintner, and so on. They were young hoodlums, always on the lookout for any mischief or violence they could get into.

"Yah!" snarled one. "It's Buckingham's wizard, so it is!"

Dr. Lambe was alarmed at their menacing appearance, but he faced them with a show of bravado. "What's in your gizzards that you provoke me, you whelps?" he demanded.

"Take us to your master, the duke," was the reply. "We've a score to settle with the cowardly skip-jack."

"Begone!" shouted Lambe in a quavering voice.

The lean and wolfish pack closed in tighter. "Why," sneered another apprentice, "the good doctor's of a waxwork complexion, as pale as that poltroon Buckingham at the Isle of Rhé. It's plain he's ailing."

A butcher's apprentice brandished his cleaver. "I'd best

open a vein, cullies," he said to the others. "There's naught like a bit of blood-letting to cure what ails a man, as the doctor himself knows."

Lambe's frantic eye fell on a group of sailors coming out of an alehouse. "Help!" he cried, beckoning them.

The sailors came up. "What's amiss, mate?" one asked.

"Protect me from these knaves!" Lambe pleaded. "I'll pay you well!"

Seeing that the doctor was well dressed, the one who had spoken nodded. "Aye, your honour, a tar-barrel's always ready to see a shipmate through a spell of slattery weather, sound as a biscuit. What say you, buckos?"

His companions nodded. They were nothing loath to make a bit of the money they saw so little of in the duke's navy.

Dr. Lambe directed them to his favourite tavern in Moorgate Street. The apprentices saw that the sailors were tougher than themselves and fell back, though they skulked a few paces behind. Others joined them as they went.

At the tavern, Dr. Lambe flung the sailors a handful of coins and they left. But to his dismay after he had dined, a vast mob was outside crying for his blood. Desperately he tried to escape, but the rioters, with a savage roar, bowled him over, trampling him underfoot. A hail of stones rained on him. Others beat him with sticks and clubs. While he could still speak, he pleaded piteously for mercy, but the only response he got was a growl: "When you see the duke, tell him we'd have done worse to him if he'd been here."

At last Dr. Lambe lay still, a tattered, bloody heap, with one of his eyes beaten out of its socket. The mob had vanished. They bore what was left of him into the nearby prison in Cheapside called the Compter. There he died the next morning.

For all Buckingham's self-assurance, he must have been alarmed when he heard of it, for he made a gesture to conciliate the people. He gave up the wardenship of the Cinque Ports. This ancient post was then an important one. The Cinque Ports were seaport cities which enjoyed certain exemptions from taxes and other privileges in return for furnishing ships to patrol the English Channel against pirates. As time passed, the wardenship became merely a much-sought-after honour, and was held three centuries later by the great Sir Winston Churchill.

Giving it up did not improve Buckingham's popularity. He was preparing to lead a second expedition against Rochelle. The Protestants there, besieged by a French army, were near starvation. The duke was as cocksure as ever that he could relieve their sufferings and thus regain the favour of Protestant England. But the people no longer had faith in him. And now ominous tales concerning him were circulating.

One told how the ghost of the duke's father, Sir George Villiers, had appeared to an old servant on the family estate. "Warn my son of his danger!" the spectre implored. "He must appease the people he has offended!"

"Wear a shirt of mail under your doublet when you go abroad," one of the duke's friends advised.

"A shirt of mail would be but a silly defence against a mob," Buckingham replied contemptuously. "As for any single man's assault, I think myself to be in no danger."

He was often at Portsmouth, where the fleet he would command was fitting out. Although there was enough money now that the subsidy had been granted, the work progressed slowly. The duke might storm and threaten, but his officers had lost all confidence in him. Their obedience was listless and slack. And the spirit of the sailors was mutinous.

During this time, a gentleman of an old English family

sat moping in lodgings he had taken in London. John Felton was a disillusioned and resentful man. He had fought well as a lieutenant in the battle on the island of Rhé. When the captain of his company was killed, he had confidently expected promotion to the vacant post. It did not come.

Felton then sought Buckingham's aid. The duke turned him down harshly and finally.

Felton had a burden of unpaid debts. He hoped to settle some of them with about £70 due him from the army. When it was not paid, his resentment toward Buckingham turned to deep hatred. Now, in his lodgings, he was reading a copy of Parliament's remonstrance against the duke. "The man is a public enemy!" he muttered.

It was August 19. Felton went out and walked to the hill which rises from where the Tower of London stands on the bank of the Thames. There, in a cutler's shop, he made a purchase. It cost him tenpence. Then he set out over the highroad leading southwestward from London. Except for a few times when friendly wagoners gave him a lift, he walked all the way to his journey's end.

At this same time Buckingham went again to Portsmouth. He took his wife with him, and they stayed at the house of the duke's friend and associate, Captain Mason.

Buckingham was out the next morning, riding in his coach through the main street of Portsmouth, which, like that of many English towns, was called the High Street. He was going to the dockyard for another try at hastening the fleet's readiness to sail.

In the brilliant summer sunshine the ramparts of the ancient fortified town lost their frowning look. The duke sniffed the bracing salt breeze blowing off the sea, pungent too with the smell of tar, of which the town reeked. Riding at anchor in the harbour were mighty ships-of-the-line and frigates mounting from a score to a hundred guns. Others lay in the dockyard for repairs or refitting.

Buckingham's spirits were buoyant, but they were chilled when the coach, approaching the Point Gate, was blocked by a crowd of sailors. "Give us the pay that's due us!" they shouted.

"Drive on," the duke ordered the coachman.

A burly sailor leaped at the door, wrenched it open and tried to drag Buckingham out of the vehicle.

"Arrest this mutineer!" cried the duke. His escort quickly seized the sailor, who was almost as quickly tried and condemned to death the next morning.

"Oh, George!" cried Buckingham's lovely duchess when he told her of it, "pray let the poor fellow go! The sailors have suffered much for want of money. I am sure he would not have dared harm you."

She pleaded so earnestly that at last her husband said, "Very well, I'll have a reprieve made out. But we must teach the fellow a lesson. We'll march him to the gibbet and let him think he's to be hanged."

The next morning, when the mutineer was taken to the gallows, an angry mob of sailors tried to rescue him. The duke sent armed horsemen galloping down on them. There was a furious melee in which two sailors were killed and others wounded.

"We cannot allow discipline to be scorned in such fashion," the duke decided. "Let the execution proceed." He tore up the reprieve and went to the gallows, tightly ringed by a force of armed men, to see the man hanged.

He rose about nine the next morning and went down to breakfast. While he was eating, Viscount Dorchester came to accompany him to a conference with the Venetian ambassador, who was trying to arrange a peace between England

and France. A few minutes later both rose to leave the dining room.

Buckingham followed Dorchester into a dark, narrow passage leading to the entrance hall of the house. Just as he reached it, a man hiding in the shadows stepped in front of him, drew a knife and plunged it into the duke's heart, crying, "God have mercy on thy soul!" It was John Felton; the knife the one he had bought on Tower Hill.

Buckingham staggered, but he had strength enough to draw out the knife and speak one word: "Villain!" Then he tottered a step or two and sank dead to the ground.

A great tumult arose. "Where is the villain?" someone demanded. "A Frenchman!" cried another.

John Felton, hiding in the kitchen, thought the second cry was, "Felton!" He called out, "Here I am."

Men were running in from all directions. Some sought to kill the murderer on the spot, but others managed to bear him off where he could be locked up. When he was examined, a note was found in the crown of his hat. It read:

"If I be slain, let no man condemn me, but rather condemn himself. It is for our sins that our hearts are hardened and become senseless, or else he had not gone so long unpunished—John Felton."

He was executed for his crime, but that could not restore Charles I's dearest friend, albeit one who had caused him trouble which had already started him on his way to the scaffold. In London, when they brought the news to the King, he flung himself on his bed with an anguished cry and wept inconsolably. But in the streets of the city the people shouted, sang and danced for joy, shouting that John Felton was a hero.

9

The Commons Rebels

Now the King had to do without his friend's guidance. He needed help, and from one direction he could already count on it. Before Buckingham's death he had brought Thomas Wentworth, intelligent, strong of character and able, over to his side.

Although Wentworth had been one of the chief advocates of the Petition of Right, he was disgusted with the endless bickering and strife in the first three Parliaments. The Yorkshire landowner, a staunch Church of England man, was also alarmed by the growing power of the Puritans in Parliament. He feared it would cause even greater chaos, perhaps even revolution.

Charles offered to make him a peer with the title of baron. Not only was Wentworth disillusioned with Parliament, but he was ambitious, and he accepted. It meant that he was back in the royal favour, would henceforth sit in the House of Lords instead of Commons and would support the King.

Charles, too, feared the Puritans. For guidance in

church matters he knew he could depend upon William Laud, Bishop of Bath and Wells. Laud was a small, red-faced man whose appearance had none of the distinction and dignity one expects of a bishop. Indeed, with his long nose and the eyes of a meddler, he looker more like what has come to be the image of the typical Puritan. Yet he was the bitterest enemy of Puritans. in all England, a strong-minded man, completely fearless. And he hated Parliament, which he always referred to as "that noise."

The highest officer of the Church of England, that of Archbishop of Canterbury, was held by George Abbot, who had strong Puritan leanings. Charles dared not dismiss Abbot, but he appointed Laud Bishop of London, the second highest church office. It was the start of Laud's rise to great power, but for his own future the King could not have made a worse mistake.

Charles decided to try again to make peace with this third Parliament when its second session began. In his speech before both houses in the Banqueting Hall of Whitehall Palace on January 24, 1629, he spoke of tonnage and poundage.

"For ever it was the gift of my people to enjoy it," he said, "and my intention in my speech at the end of the last session was not to challenge tonnage and poundage as of right, but of necessity, by which I was to take it until you had granted it unto me."

But the House of Commons did not grasp the olive branch the King had held out by saying he had not intended to claim that Parliament had no control over tonnage and poundage. When a number of merchants refused to pay it, their goods had been seized by the King's agents. What infuriated the Commons most was that one of its own members, John Rolle, was among them.

Such seizures, Sir Robert Phelips told the Commons, were in violation of the Petition of Right. "Cast your eyes about," he added, "and you shall see violations on all sides."

Sir John Eliot drew up a resolution against the King's collection of tonnage and poundage. Charles, learning of it, lost no time in trying to keep it from coming to a vote. On March 2 Sir John Finch, the Speaker of the House of Commons and a friend of the King, rose and said he had a message from the Crown. "It is his Majesty's pleasure," he said, "that the House of Commons be adjourned to March 10."

Instantly shouts of "No! No!" rose from all sides. Eliot then asked the Speaker to read the resolution.

"I have an absolute command from his Majesty to leave the chair if anyone attempts to speak," said Finch, and he started to do so.

Two members leaped from their seats, seized his arms and thrust him back into the chair. Several members of the King's Privy Council who were in the hall managed to free Finch and he darted for the door. A crowd of members blocked the way.

The two who had first seized Finch grabbed him again and pushed him back into his seat. " 'Swounds!" growled one, "you shall sit till we please to rise."

The House of Commons was in pandemonium. At last the Speaker rose and said, "I know of no instance in which the House has continued to transact business after a command from his Majesty to adjourn. What would any of you do if you were in my place?" His voice quavered. "Let not my desire to serve you faithfully be my ruin!"

"We shall be ready to adjourn after the declaration has been read," said Eliot. "If you refuse to obey, you shall be called before the bar of the House to explain your actions."

At this open defiance of the King's command, a number

of members who were friendly to the Crown rose to leave.

"Bar the doors!" came a shout. A member closed and locked them and put the key in his pocket.

Finch was weeping. "Let me go to the King!" he cried. "If I do not return speedily, tear me in pieces!"

John Selden said to him, "Dare you not, Mr. Speaker, put the question when we command you? If you will not put it, we must sit still; thus we shall never be able to do anything."

"I will not say I shall not put the reading of the paper to the question," Finch replied in a broken voice, "but I must say I dare not."

At last, hot-tempered John Eliot threw the declaration into the fire which crackled on the hearth that winter's day. Just then there was a knock on the door. It was Black Rod, bearing a message. Charles had learned of the riot and was sending his royal guard to break down the doors and disperse the House of Commons.

Denzil Holles, one of those who had forced the Speaker back into his chair, had read Eliot's declaration before the session began. He told the members what it said: Anyone who voluntarily paid tonnage and poundage unless it were granted by Parliament, or who advised anyone else to pay it, was an enemy of the country.

Holles put it to the Commons for a vote. It was passed with roars of "Aye! Aye!" Then the House voted to adjourn.

On March 10 the King went in high dudgeon to the House of Lords, wearing his robes of state and his crown. He did not even bother to summon the House of Commons there, though a number of its members came.

"I thought it necessary to come here today," he told the Lords, "to declare to you and all the world that it was merely the undutiful and seditious carriage of the Lower

House that hath made the dissolution of this Parliament. You, my lords, are so far from being any cause of it that I take as much comfort in your dutiful demeanour as I am justly distasted with their proceedings."

As for the House of Commons, the King's bitterness was against those who had led the opposition to his desires. "Let me tell you," he went on, "it is far from me to adjudge all the House alike guilty, it being so few vipers among them that did cast the mist of undutifulness over most of their eyes. As those vipers must look for their punishment, so you, my lords, must justly expect from me that favour and protection that a good king oweth to his loving and faithful subjects."

And with that he dissolved his third Parliament. One of his friends who saw him when he returned from the House of Lords remarked that he looked pleased, as though some great weight had been lifted from his mind.

The King was determined that those responsible for the riot in the House of Commons should suffer the severest penalties. Eliot, Holles, and five others who had taken leading parts were seized and imprisoned. While Charles was making up his mind what their punishment should be, the seven languished in the Tower of London. At last, on May 6, they applied to the court of the King's Bench for writs of *habeas corpus.*

Habeas corpus had grown out of the famous clause of Magna Carta: "No free man shall be taken or imprisoned or disseized [his property taken from him] or exiled or in any way destroyed . . . except by the lawful judgment of his peers and by the law of the land." The words mean "produce the body." When such a writ is issued for a man in prison, he must be produced in court and allowed to go free on bail.

The King's Bench was one of the four great courts which sat in Westminster Hall. It dealt with offences concerning both the King and his subjects. Charles summoned its twelve judges and asked what they thought of the case. Seven of them were against him. But the King found a way of silencing them. When the day came for the prisoners' appearance before the King's Bench under the writs of *habeas corpus*, none were there. Charles had ordered the keeper of the Tower not to let them out.

This only put off the day of reckoning, however. Now the King decided the prisoners should be freed on bail if they liked—at a price. They must first ask his pardon for what they had done. And they must post a bond of money to ensure their good behaviour while they were free and awaiting trial.

All refused to apologize or post the bond. It was clear to the judges that under the law they had to grant bail whether or not the prisoners complied with the King's terms. Yet he had appointed them and could be rid of them if he pleased.

Finally, the three who had been the principal leaders in disobeying the King—Eliot, Holles and Benjamin Valentine—were brought to trial. The judges now saw things the way the King did, and the men were found guilty. Eliot was fined £2000, Holles £1000, and Valentine £500. They were also ordered to acknowledge their guilt and post a good-behaviour bond.

Holles and Valentine obeyed, and all the prisoners were released in time except Eliot, who was unyielding. The King ordered him back to the Tower.

Charles had made up his mind that he would summon no more Parliaments. As for the means of raising money in the future, he and his advisers had some ideas about that.

First, the King ordered that all who refused to pay tonnage and poundage should be imprisoned until he directed their release. But tonnage and poundage alone could not keep England going.

Charles then decided to put the ancient forest laws back in force. They forbade the people to poach in the vast royal forests by hunting the wild animals there, to take wood from them or to clear the land and occupy it. Magna Carta had had something to say about the forest laws. It required that an investigation be made of "all evil customs" connected with the laws and that such customs be abolished.

Little had been done to carry this out, but gradually many of the forest laws' provisions had fallen into disuse, although they had never been repealed. Large parts of great landowners' estates were royal forest which had been cleared. Even whole villages had sprung up in what once had been woodland. Charles decided to impose heavy fines, provided under these laws, upon all who were using what had been royal forest.

Another even more profitable scheme was ship money. There was nothing new about it. Rulers of England in earlier centuries had used this tax to provide money to build ships for the navy. It had been levied on the seaport towns, since they profited most by having their sea trade protected against enemy navies and privateers in wartime, and pirates in peacetime.

In the past the seaports had always paid ship money without too much grumbling. But now the King proposed to obtain even more revenue by this means. All over England, towns and villages also profited by exporting wool, coal, salt, cloth and a host of other products. Why should they not pay ship money too? Charles issued a decree that all must do so.

Next, one of the King's advisers suggested the granting of monopolies. For example, a manufacturer of soap would be granted the sole right to make it in England. In return he would pay the King a certain amount for every pound of soap he produced. It was a vicious practice, since it could put other makers of such products out of business, but it would surely aid in filling the royal coffers.

By all these measures, the King expected to have enough money to run the country. Nevertheless, it would not be enough to wage expensive war against England's two enemies, Spain and France. Soon after Parliament had been dissolved, a peace was patched up with France, eagerly aided by Queen Henrietta. The following year a peace treaty was signed with Spain.

Charles was now confident that he could do very well without Parliament. He would go on alone and rule England himself without interference with the royal prerogative. His troubles were over. So he thought.

10

The Rule of the King

Hearing a trumpet blast in the distance, the guard at the head of the pack train plodding over the Great North Road peered ahead, squinting in the brilliant sunlight. At first he saw only a cloud of dust in the distance; then he made out mounted horsemen before and behind a coach approaching from the north.

He turned and shouted an order to the other guards strung out along the single file of thirty pack horses with their heavy loads of goods. The train veered off the road. Its attendants knew better than to dispute the right of way with some great lord and his escort. The bells on the horses' girth straps stopped jingling and the animals stood patiently, glad of a chance to browse at the edge of the bleak Northumberland moor.

Those who were with the pack train eyed the cavalcade curiously as it passed, aware that a personage of more than ordinary consequence must be inside the coach. It glittered in splendour, its four horses were regally caparisoned, the riders of its escort elegantly uniformed and heavily armed.

From within the coach, King Charles glanced out idly at the pack train and then settled back on the cushions, which gave little protection against the constant lurching and jolting over the miserable road with its many potholes. His joints were sore already, and his journey from Berwick to London no more than begun. Alnwick Castle would be a welcome sight at the end of this first day's journey. Nor was the King's mind any easier than his body, for he was full of trouble on this day in June, 1639.

Everything had been going so well until the Scots had revolted. England had prospered in the ten years since Charles had dissolved his third Parliament. He had got along nicely without another one.

The revolt had arisen over a prayer book, of all things, though its origin really went back to the time when his father had been King James VI of Scotland. By appointing bishops who would carry out his ideas, James had gradually introduced parts of the Church of England service into the Presbyterian Church, or Kirk, of Scotland. But it was not until Charles's reign over both countries that the Scots had protested violently.

As his coach rolled on, Charles thought of the riots that had taken place there.

On the morning of July 28, 1637, in Edinburgh, the members of the King's council for Scotland marched in a procession to St. Giles's Cathedral. It was a historic occasion, marking the first time the new prayer book of the Church of England, drawn up by the Archbishop of Canterbury and four compliant Scottish bishops, had been used in the Kirk of Scotland.

The members of the council were compliant men too. Charles had seen to it that none of the great and powerful

Scottish lords who might oppose his will were included.

If any of the council were worried on this fine mid-summer Sunday, they showed no sign of it. True, John Stewart, Lord Traquair, was not present. Traquair had discovered business which took him all the way across to the western part of Scotland. And although Archibald Campbell, Lord Lorne, was a tough chieftain who had subdued the ferocious clans of Macdonald and MacGregor in the wild mountains to the north, he had fallen suddenly ill today.

The austere cathedral was so full that the crowd had overflowed around the entrance. As the council entered, the pews were filled with mute, dour and craggy-faced Scots who sat like the graven images so abhorred by good Presbyterians. In the rear, jam-packed latecomers stood, or sat on folding chairs.

The dignified council took seats held for it at the front of the church. Then the tombstone-faced dean of the cathedral rose to begin the service with the new prayer book.

Suddenly a tempest of yells and catcalls shook the stout arched beams of the nave's dome overhead. Nice-looking old ladies in their decent Sunday best screeched dreadful imprecations. All at once, Bibles hurled by the congregation were flying through the air, followed by the folding chairs of those in the rear. The dean ducked behind his pulpit. In their pews the council members cowered under the full force of the barrage.

The council's stalwart guards seized the leaders of the riot and hustled them outside. Order was restored, and the congregation sat sullenly while the service continued, constantly interrupted by a hubbub of shouts from outside, hammering on the locked doors and the clack of stones striking the cathedral windows.

The angry King struck back with a royal command: the

leaders of the riot must be arrested and sentenced for their
crime. And the prayer book must continue to be used.

A number of Scottish lords and staunch Presbyterian
clergymen resolved to fight the King's edict. They drew up
a document which they called the National Covenant. It
stated that the Presbyterian faith was forever established as
the sole religion of Scotland.

In the churchyard of Greyfriars Kirk in Edinburgh, on
February 28, 1638, the Covenant was placed on a flat tomb-
stone. All that day, Wednesday, and the next, the gentry and
ministers of Edinburgh filed into the churchyard to sign it.
On Friday the rest of the people, young and old, came.
Then, all over the Lowlands of Scotland, the kirks were
filled with long lines of men, women and children putting
their names to the Covenant.

The occasion was called "the great marriage day of the
nation with God." Southern Scotland was now united against
the King.

Now the King's coach crossed the River Tyne and entered the Black Country. Off to the east a great, untidy cloud
of smoke billowed lazily into the summer sky. It hung over
Shields, at the river's mouth, where the immense salt works
burned coal from the mines of Durham County.

The villages, above the labyrinth of shafts and passages
of the coal pits deep in the earth, were untidy too, grimy eye-
sores with their narrow streets and the sooty, squalid hovels
of the miners. The people's faces were dark—not only per-
manently smutted with coal dust but gloomy with the despair
of poverty, in which they lived from birth to the grave.

The King gave no more than a passing thought to these
wretched folk. He felt a responsibility for his subjects, and
in his way he loved them, but he simply did not want to be

bothered with their troubles. It was the same with his rule of England. If only Parliament would let him enjoy the ancient privileges of a king, he would be content to leave the rest of the tedious job of government to its members.

What Charles wanted most was the leisure to gratify his passion for art. Already his collection was one of the finest in all Europe. Indeed, it almost seemed that the King loved his art collection more than his children, for he spent less time with them. Charles, Prince of Wales and heir to the throne, was now nine years old. The other children, Mary, James and Elizabeth, ranged from eight down to four. From their early childhood they had been under the care of tutors and governesses, and their parents did not see a great deal of them.

At this moment during his journey, the King's mind was occupied with the greatest of his troubles—the Scots and what had happened at Berwick when he arrived with his army to put down the rebellion in Scotland.

The 20,000 men of Charles's army, camped in the meadows on the English side of the Tweed near Berwick, were discontented, uncomfortable and hungry. For more than a month they had waited, and nothing had happened. Most of them were herdsmen and farmhands. They had marched unwillingly in companies raised by the lords whose tenants they were. Now, in June, they were much needed at home, what with the crops and stock to be tended and hay soon to be cut.

The weather in this northern shire of Northumberland was abominable. Day after day, thunderheads piled up and violent storms drenched the camp. When they passed, the men's wet clothes steamed under a sun hot enough to fry eggs.

It was a rabble of an army, short of everything it needed to fight. Its weapons were pikes, spears, bows and arrows, antiquated muskets. It was poorly trained; many of the soldiers did not know how to fire a gun. It did not have enough to eat. And there was no indication as to when, if ever, the men would be paid.

The worst thing was that it was an army without a purpose. Most of the soldiers cared not a whit what sort of prayer book was used in the Scottish Kirk. If there was a battle they would fight if they could not flee, but their hearts were not in it.

Across the Tweed in Scotland the Scottish army was camped. It was also 20,000 strong, but it was superior in several ways. Its soldiers too came mostly from farms, but they were a tougher breed, so used to the freakish weather of the north that they hardly noticed its discomforts. They were better trained, equipped and fed too, for their leaders had seen to that. These men, accustomed to hunting deer in the Scottish wilds, were good shots with a musket and deadly with the pike.

The greatest difference was that the Scots had something to fight for. They bitterly resented the attempt to dictate the way they worshipped. The soldiers had been brought up in God-fearing Presbyterian families. They would have no other form of religion.

Morning and night the Scots' voices were raised in the singing of psalms. Sometimes they chanted prayers in unison. And there was the wild, shrill skirl of bagpipes and the scraping of fiddlers who played to hearten the army. The Scottish companies' banners were emblazoned in gold with the words: "For Christ's Cross and the Covenant."

The English army was beaten before a shot had been

fired, and if the soldiers did not know it, their leaders did. In the well-appointed tent of the Earl of Arundel, the inept English commander, six Covenanter leaders were discussing terms of peace with Charles and his councillors.

They faced each other stiffly at first. The King's manner was aloof, though he had little to be haughty about. The Covenanters were quietly respectful. They had every advantage in this parley; yet, after all, Charles was, like his father, a Scot, born at Dunfermline Castle. He had been crowned King of Scotland in Edinburgh in 1633.

They were speaking of how the Church Assembly of Scotland had excommunicated the bishops who had tried to force the new prayer book upon them. The King addressed a question to one of the Covenanters: "Pray tell me, Lord Rothes, would your Assembly take it upon itself to excommunicate me, the King of Scots?"

John Leslie, Earl of Rothes, could be tough when it was necessary, but he was also a skilled politician. As a good Presbyterian too, he knew his Bible and the verse of Proverbs which says, "A soft answer turneth away wrath."

"Sir," he said, "you are so good a King that you would not deserve it, but if I were King and should offend, I think the Church of Scotland might excommunicate me."

Charles gave Rothes one of his rare smiles. After that his manner was more amiable. But one of the Covenanters, Archibald Johnson, Laird of Warriston, was a narrow-minded fanatic where his religion was concerned. Sometimes his outbursts seemed like those of a madman.

"I like not these offers of the King," he told his colleagues, "nor do I trust them."

At this insolence the King's expression hardened, but he spoke calmly: "If a treaty of peace between us is signed,

I will call a Scottish Parliament. It and your Assembly shall discuss the future of your church."

"He is playing for time!" Warriston cried. "Whatever may be decided, he will overrule it!"

The King's eyes flashed. "The Devil himself could not make a more uncharitable interpretation of my offer," he snapped.

But Warriston was right. Charles was playing for time. He had not retreated from his determination to force the new prayer book upon Scotland. But if he could obtain a truce, he might somehow find the money to raise and equip a decent army.

He won this objective. A treaty known as the Pacification of Berwick was signed in the camp on June 19, 1639. Both armies were to disband. The King agreed to come to Scotland in the fall for the sessions of the Scottish Parliament and Assembly.

Yet the Covenanter leaders knew the delay would aid them too. More and more Englishmen were turning each day toward their cause and against the King. Also, they might enlist the aid of several European powers who wished England no good.

Thus, what is known as the First Bishops' War came to a peaceful end—but the peace was uneasy.

The countryside looked more prosperous as the Great North Road traversed the rolling wolds, or plains, of Yorkshire. The green carpet of lush grass was patched with the white of grazing herds of sheep. Their wool provided a livelihood for the weavers in the towns and revenue for the kingdom from the fine broadcloth for which England was famous.

Riding with Charles now was his nephew Prince Rupert,

son of his sister Elizabeth and the Elector Frederick. The
young man, arriving at Berwick from Holland just after the
King had left, had caught up with him at Durham. The Elector had died, and his son had come to plead for money to
continue efforts to recover the Palatinate. But the King could
give him no encouragement.

Now Charles's thoughts turned again to the ten years
of prosperity since the last Parliament. Money had flowed
into the treasury from tonnage and poundage and the three
ship money levies which had enabled him to put the navy
back into fighting trim. Fines had been imposed upon rich
nobles who had encroached on the royal forests. And the
monopolies the King had created produced a rich harvest for
his purse.

Of course, there had been resistance at first. Some of
the inland towns had revolted, insisting such measures were
illegal. Banbury was one, with its large population of Puritans who were opposed to the King. Charles's lip curled as
he thought of how it was said that Banbury's stiff-necked
and bigoted Puritans hanged their cats on Monday for vio-
lating the Sabbath by catching mice on that day.

The John Hampden case had put a stop to refusals to
pay ship money. The King's old enemy in Parliament had
been assessed a paltry twenty shillings on a small piece of
his landholdings. When he refused to pay he had been haled
into court.

The King found out that five of the eight judges would
vote in Hampden's favour. So he had the case transferred to
the Exchequer Chamber, a kind of court of appeals. Here
he had won—though just barely, by a vote of seven to five.
But it was enough. His collection of ship money was legal,
and the resistance to it subsided.

There had been outraged protests from the vintners, salt

producers and soapmakers over the monopolies too. Especially soap. That ridiculous business in Bristol . . .

On Saturday, October 5, 1633, it seemed that most of Bristol's 20,000 people had somehow wedged themselves into the City Cross, where Wine, Corn, Bread and High streets met. The word had spread that the great soap test was to be held that day.

The King had granted a monopoly to some London soapmakers for fourteen years. In return for paying him £4 for each ton they produced, they were allowed to examine all other soap made in the kingdom. If it were not as good as theirs they could seize or destroy it. That was the purpose of the London soapmakers' agent, Captain Conningsbye, in coming to Bristol.

The city was alarmed. Next to its seaport on the Avon River, soapmaking was its most important source of revenue. If its soap were found inferior to the London product, the soapmakers' trade would be wiped out, and with it the jobs of many people.

They had set up a platform in the Cross, with two washtubs on it. Servants from the nearby Rose Tavern were dumping piggins of steaming water into them. On a table there were two piles of soiled napkins from the tavern and some of the Bristol and London soaps. Nine witnesses, including Captain Conningsbye, were on the platform.

When all was ready, the two laundresses flounced forward. Representing London was Elizabeth Delahy; for Bristol it was Sara Willis. Sara glared belligerently at her opponent, who responded with a contemptuous toss of her head. Then the two plumped their napkins into the tubs, added soap, and set to work.

Sara went at it so furiously that it was as if she had the other laundress by the hair in the tub and was trying to shake her teeth out as she swished and pummeled and scrubbed. The breathless crowd cheered her. When the washing was done, wrung out and draped on a line stretched for the purpose, the witnesses crowded forward.

"*Mine's* the cleanest!" cried Elizabeth Delahy.

"She lies!" screeched Sara. "Anyone with half an eye can see mine's the cleanest—and sweetest!"

She snatched a napkin off the line and shoved it under Captain Conningsbye's nose. "Smell!" Then she pointed to the table. "I've used less soap too—look!"

It was true. She had used only part of her soap. And after the witnesses had inspected and smelled of both contestants' work, they agreed that Bristol had won. Even Captain Conningsbye grudgingly admitted that at least there was no difference.

It did not do Bristol any good, however. Soon afterward, the King ordered seven of the city's soap-boiling works closed. The townspeople became more enraged with the King than before.

As the King approached London, the towns and villages were closer together, set like the counters on a vast checkerboard of small farms with neat gardens where all manner of vegetables were raised for the tables of the great metropolis. Charles was absorbed in the problems with which he had soon to come to grips. As never before in his reign, he needed help.

He could depend upon William Laud, of course, for counsel and support on religious questions. When George Abbot, the Archbishop of Canterbury, died in 1633, Charles had appointed Laud in his place as head of the Church of England and had leaned heavily on him in his struggle against the Puritans.

The King liked and trusted the little prelate who was devoted to him and so fanatically determined that the Church of England should be all-powerful in the kingdom. But there were clergymen, as well as their congregations, who felt there should be changes to make the service and the churches more attractive. Some introduced music, some put candles on the altar, others even set up images of the Virgin Mary and the saints.

Laud bitterly opposed these innovations, which smacked of the Church of Rome. He used an ecclesiastical court, the High Commission, to prosecute those who made such changes. He sent out clergy of his staff to snoop and spy on erring ministers and their flocks. These "visitations," as they were called, stirred much resentment all over England against Laud and the bishops who did his bidding. And the archbishop had been foremost in trying to impose the new prayer book upon the Presbyterians of Scotland.

Laud was less ruthless against the Catholics. For one thing, he had Queen Henrietta to reckon with. Being a devout Catholic, she opposed all efforts to persecute them, using her strong influence over her husband. In fact, relations between the Church of England, which had sprung from the Catholic, and the Vatican in Rome were quite cordial.

Laud fought the Puritans without mercy, however. He suppressed their ministers, broke up their secret meetings and ferreted out the chaplains some Puritans kept hidden in their homes to conduct services. Many Puritans left England, migrating to New England and other parts of the infant American colonies.

The Puritans who remained were as determined to preserve their church as Laud was to destroy it. All the archbishop's efforts could not keep the Puritan power from growing. The King did not understand that this power was a sinister threat to him.

He was thinking now of another of Laud's measures against the Puritans—the suppression of books and pamphlets they printed criticizing the Church of England and supporting their own. Charles wondered why the severe punishments meted out to some Puritans had had so little effect. That given to William Prynne and the two other writers of Puritan pamphlets, for example . . .

The sun beat down pitilessly upon the pavement of the Palace Yard in Westminster on June 30, 1637. But the crowd which had wedged itself in there gave no thought to its discomfort. It was too excited over one of the favourite sports of Londoners—watching fellow human beings suffer barbaric punishment.

All eyes were fixed on the scaffold there in the Palace Yard. The executioner, a man with a brutal face, was putting Prynne, Henry Burton and John Bastwick into the pillories mounted on it. The pillory was a wooden panel fixed to an upright and made in two sections, with three holes bored in its centre, one larger than the others. The executioner raised the upper section, put the prisoner's head and hands through the lower halves of the holes, then lowered the upper part, locking the man securely into the pillory while he stood on the scaffold.

Persons standing in the pillory were ordinarily greeted with abuse and a hail of rotten eggs, spoiled fruit, sticks and stones. But today some in the crowd tossed sweet-smelling bunches of rosemary and herbs at the three men's feet, and others ascended the scaffold and held cups of wine to their mouths.

In spite of the heat, no one moved away during the two hours the prisoners stood there. The most exciting part of the show was yet to come. Meanwhile, the three men made speeches. Prynne, who had been a barrister and was accustomed to lecturing juries in court, spoke longest and loudest. The crowd cheered as he charged that an Englishman's liberty had been violated by his conviction.

When the speeches were done, silence fell over the Palace Yard as the executioner stepped up to Prynne. A knife glittered in his hand.

A dismal moan rose from the crowd. The executioner had begun to cut off one of Prynne's ears, but instead of severing it with a clean stroke, he was hacking it off. The prisoner cried out and writhed helplessly in the grip of the pillory; blood streamed down the side of his face and neck.

" 'E's doing it a-purpose, Jack Ketch is," one onlooker growled to his neighbour.

"I'll lay you a shilling 'e's foxed with ale," replied the other.

"Nah!" said the first man. "Ketch knows wot 'e's about, all right. 'E's in a fusty 'umor, 'e is. Prynne didn't give 'im but 'arf a crown."

There may have been no truth in this gossip that Prynne had not tipped the executioner enough to ensure gentler treatment, but the removal of his ears, in accordance with the Star Chamber's sentence, was a long, bloody and agonizing piece of butchery.

When the ears of all three prisoners had been removed, there remained one final humiliation for Prynne. From a brazier in which a coal fire glowed, the executioner drew a red-hot branding iron with a pair of tongs. Those nearest the scaffold heard it sizzle and saw a wisp of smoke rise as the letters SL (Seditious Libeler) were burned into the bloodstained Prynne's forehead.

When the three men were freed from the pillories to begin their journey to prison for the rest of their lives, a great yell burst from the spectators. It was a protest and a threat, raised against Archbishop Laud and his ruthless vengeance upon all who dared oppose his religious principles. The King, if he had heard the roar in nearby Whitehall Palace, might have done well to heed its portent.

As the royal coach entered London, the King's mind was easier. Wentworth would soon be with him. Before leaving Berwick, he had summoned him home from Ireland. "Come when you will, you shall be welcome," Charles had written.

In 1633 the King had sent this strongest and ablest of his supporters to govern Ireland. Wentworth had held the fiercely independent people of that rebellious island in check, prevailed upon the Irish Parliament to make good laws, suppressed corrupt government, and carried out his duties with a stern but efficient hand. He had developed the growing of flax and its manufacture into fine linen, relieving to some extent the terrible poverty there.

With Wentworth by his side, the King would have less to fear from a decision he had reached. At first he had resisted the advice of some of his councillors, who said the only way to wage the inevitable war with the Scots was to summon another Parliament to grant the money he would need. Now he had made up his mind to do so.

Some of his old enemies would be missing from this Parliament. Sir Edward Coke had died. So had the bitterest of his foes—Sir John Eliot. There was no pity in the King's heart as he thought of what had happened. Eliot had chosen to remain a prisoner in the Tower of London rather than admit his fault for his part in the uprising of the 1629 Parliament. In 1632 he had fallen seriously ill. At last he sent a petition to the King, asking his release so that he might recover.

Charles remembered the grudging way in which Eliot had written. "His petition is not humble enough," he had said.

So Eliot had continued to waste away in the Tower. On November 27, 1633, he had died.

Plenty were left, however, to continue Parliament's struggle to put an end to the divine right of kings. Among them were Pym, Hampden, Holles and a Puritan of whom little had been heard as yet—Oliver Cromwell. As he thought of these men, Charles was glad he had Thomas Wentworth on his side. In the difficult times ahead, Wentworth would be the rock on which the King's strength would rest. He would not forget it; Wentworth should be rewarded.

11

The Scots Strike

The King did not forget his vow. In January, 1640, he made Thomas Wentworth the first Earl of Strafford. Thereafter, according to English custom, he was no longer known as Wentworth but as Strafford.

Strafford did not remain long in England after his return from Ireland. Following the Pacification of Berwick, the Scottish Parliament and the Assembly of the Kirk both voted to abolish the Church of England in Scotland forever. At this defiance, Charles began again to prepare for war. He had summoned a new Parliament to meet in April, hoping it would grant him the money to bring the Scots to their knees. Now he sent Strafford back to Ireland to raise an army which would join the English, and to ask the Irish Parliament for money.

Strafford had no such troubles with his Parliaments in Ireland as Charles did with his in England. In Dublin, the Irish Parliament welcomed the earl joyfully and sent a message to the King thanking him for giving them "so just, wise, vigilant and profitable a governor." They promptly agreed to raise an army of 9000 to fight the Scottish Covenanters, whom they hated, and to grant the King £180,000. In a little over a week, Strafford was ready to start back to England.

He arrived just after the English Parliament opened on April 13, 1640. Whatever hopes the King had of getting along with this first one in eleven years were soon dashed.

Charles made only a short speech, leaving it to the Lord Keeper of the House of Lords to make his wants known. The King's enemies bristled, for this was none other than John Finch, the hapless Speaker of the 1629 Parliament. Finch faced them arrogantly, for he had gone far since then.

As chief justice of the court which tried William Prynne, he had pronounced the brutal sentence. And he had also pronounced judgment upon John Hampden for refusing to pay ship money, saying, "Acts of Parliament to take away the King's power in the defence of his kingdom are void."

Now, having been made a baron, he was presiding over the House of Lords. He all but licked Charles's boots as he spoke. England had the best king in its history, he said, and the most virtuous queen, while their children gave promise of the same excellence. As for the rebellion in Scotland, it was unspeakably wicked. A subsidy to put it down must be voted at once, as well as the right to collect tonnage and poundage. These things done, his Majesty would graciously consider Parliament's grievances.

Parliament would have none of this. In place of Eliot, John Pym had become the King's most implacable enemy. He launched a savage attack on Charles's actions and those of his supporters in the eleven years that had elapsed.

He said the treatment of those who had led the 1629 uprising, as well as the sudden dissolution of Parliament, were illegal. So were the King's continued collection of tonnage and poundage without a grant from Parliament, his imposition of the ship money levies, the creation of monopolies and the fines levied under the old forest laws. All these grievances must be settled before a subsidy was voted.

When Strafford arrived from Ireland, he gave Charles some advice: "I suggest that you go to the House of Lords, your Majesty, and ask them to declare that the subsidy should be taken up first."

The Lords supported the King by voting in favour of this proposal. But Strafford's advice had not been good, for the House of Commons was now enraged against the King. It drew up a petition demanding that he make a lasting peace with the Scots. Before a vote could be taken on it, the King hurried to the House of Lords and dissolved Parliament. This one became famous as the Short Parliament. It had lasted just 22 days.

Once more the King faced the problem of obtaining money to fight a war which had already begun, for Scottish rebels had fired on the royal garrison in Edinburgh Castle. Again Strafford gave Charles advice: "Let the City of London be required to lend your Majesty £100,000. Let ship money be collected with all necessary force. That will provide enough money for a short campaign. I am sure the Scots can be beaten quickly."

Charles not only accepted this counsel, but doubled the demand upon the City to £200,000. When the loan was refused, four of the aldermen, who with the Lord Mayor governed the City, were put in prison. But this stirred such an uproar in the City that they were released and the loan was abandoned.

The King suspected that some of his enemies in the late Parliament were plotting against him with the Scots.

He had three members of the House of Lords and three of the Commons—the Earl of Warwick, Lord Brooke, Lord Saye, Pym, Hampden and Sir Walter Erle—arrested and sent to the Tower. Their homes were then ransacked for evidence, but nothing was found.

Their imprisonment helped to touch off an explosion. Hatred against the King and his supporters was rising in London. Journeymen and apprentices, always ready for mischief, were especially incensed. The King's monopolies had put many of them out of work. They were afraid, too, that they would be impressed by force into the royal army. They did not want to fight, because they felt the Scots were right in demanding freedom to worship as they pleased. They blamed Archbishop Laud for the trouble in Scotland.

On May 11 a riot erupted across the Thames in the boroughs of Blackfriars and Southwark. There, as if by magic, an angry group of apprentices and journeymen gathered. One had a drum on which he beat a long roll.

Others heard it and tumbled out of the houses. Along the teeming waterfront of London, a crowd of sailors joined the rioters. Soon the mob grew to five hundred or more, armed with clubs, sticks and marlinspikes. With a roar it charged into Lambeth, just upriver. There stood ancient Lambeth Palace, London headquarters of the Archbishop of Canterbury.

Laud heard them coming. He sneaked out of the palace and was rowed across the river to safety in Whitehall Palace. When the mob reached Lambeth Palace, its door was bolted. A seaman sent a crowbar crashing down on it. By that time a force of constables had arrived. They seized the ringleaders and hauled them off to jail. The rest of the mob followed, battered its way inside and set the others free.

There was a furious battle as the constables tried to

recapture their prisoners. Meanwhile, the King had ordered
the Lord Mayor to call out the City's trained bands, a kind
of volunteer militia. When word of their coming reached
the mob, it melted away and vanished.

The King was sure the members of Parliament he had
put in the Tower were responsible. The man who had beaten
the drum was vainly tortured in the hope that he would
confess something. The sailor who had wielded the crowbar
was hanged and quartered, and his head impaled on a spike
on London Bridge with those of other malefactors which
always adorned the bridge in those days. London did not
forget the King's barbaric revenge.

With the Scots threatening to invade England at any
moment, Charles did not know which way to turn. Ship
money was barely dribbling in. Some of the officials charged
with collecting it dared not risk their lives trying to do so.
Often, if a landowner refused to pay his share and his property was seized, his friends and tenants forced its return.

The City of London was one of the most rebellious
parts of the kingdom. It resolutely refused to pay ship money.
A command that it raise 4000 men for the new army was
ignored.

In desperation, Charles asked both Spain and France
for loans. They refused. Queen Henrietta appealed to the
Vatican for money. The Pope replied that he would help if
Charles would become a Catholic, but that the King would
not do.

There was trouble beyond measure in the new army.
All over the kingdom the soldiers, who were forced to serve,
rioted and revolted. They burned fences, set fire to buildings,
invaded jails and set the prisoners free and burst into Archbishop Laud's Episcopal churches and wrecked them.

The King heard that the Scottish army had three times

as many men as the one in the previous war, better artillery and better equipment. And Holland was sending shiploads of arms, which eluded the royal navy's blockade of the coast and were smuggled into Scotland.

But he refused to believe these things. His general at Newcastle, near the Scottish border in Northumberland, was Lord Conway, a remarkably incompetent man. He told Charles the Scots had practically no army. That was enough for the ostrichlike King, whose head was buried in the sand of what he chose to believe. He also chose to believe that his own army was quite capable of giving the Scots a sound beating.

Suddenly Conway sang a different tune. He sent an urgent message to London: the Scots were about to cross the border with an army so strong that he could not hold Newcastle.

"I will go north to be with the army," the King announced, and on August 20 he set out for York. On the way, more bad news reached him. The English commander in chief, the Earl of Northumberland, was ill. There were those who whispered that the earl's ailment was convenient, since he knew military disaster lay ahead, and that he would be blamed for it if he continued active command.

Strafford was about to leave for Ireland to bring over the 9000 troops which had been raised there. The King appointed him commander in chief and ordered him to come north instead.

Strafford was no military expert, though for that matter neither was Northumberland, who had previously been Lord High Admiral. But Strafford was a leader; he had great self-confidence, and he could get things done.

His first action was to send Conway a sharp reprimand, telling him to stand and fight the Scots. He also told him to use his whole force of 12,000 men to keep the enemy from crossing the River Tyne. Then he started north for Selby in Yorkshire, where the main English army of about 12,000 was camped. Perhaps if he could have set out earlier he might somehow have staved off disaster. But before he was well on his way, the Scots reached the Tyne.

It was the story of Berwick all over again, but worse. Strafford's orders did not arrive in time, and Conway divided his force, leaving two-thirds of it at Newcastle, which was impossible to defend. The rest, about 3000 infantry and 1000 cavalry, he placed on the south bank of the Tyne where the Scots would have to cross, upriver from Newcastle.

The Scottish commander had one of his cannons dismantled and carried to the top of a church tower near the crossing. There it was reassembled, and it began hurling cannonballs into the midst of Conway's force across the river. When the raw English soldiers heard the terrifying screech and whoosh of the balls and saw how they cut men to pieces, they were panic-stricken.

Only a few Scots could swarm across the shallow ford before the tide, rushing up from the nearby river mouth, blocked the passage of the rest. But although the English cavalry charged the invaders as they came ashore, the aim of the Scottish musketeers was deadly. The horsemen turned and galloped to the rear, causing complete confusion in the ranks of the infantry behind them. Then Conway's entire force fled. It was a shameful, humiliating rout.

The fainthearted Conway then marched the rest of his army out of Newcastle, leaving it to the enemy. The Scottish army pursued the retreating English as far as the River Tees. They were now in possession of both Northumberland and Durham counties. The people there received them well, especially when the Scots kept their promise not to take so much as a chicken or a pot of ale without paying for it in cash.

It took a great deal to shake Strafford's self-confidence, but now he was in the depths of despair. He wrote to a friend: "Pity me, for never came any man to so lost a business. The army unprovided of all necessaries. That part which I bring with me from Durham the worst I ever saw . . . the country from Berwick to York in the power of the Scots. . . . God of his goodness deliver me out of this, the greatest evil of my life."

As for the downcast King, still more woe lay just ahead. He had had to free Pym, Hampden and the others he had suspected of plotting against him; now they joined with a number of nobles and influential men in drawing up a petition to Charles. It listed all the grievances which had been discussed in the Short Parliament, and demanded a new Parliament which would bring to trial those who were responsible for these ills.

The King would probably not have yielded, but for a similar petition which was circulated in London and signed by 10,000 persons. Ten thousand signatures—and the victorious Scots poised to sweep on toward London, which in its resentment against him would surely receive them joyfully. Charles agreed to summon another Parliament, and he invited the Scots to peace negotiations.

They were willing to negotiate. For one thing, they had no wish to undertake the tremendous job of subduing England or to humiliate the King any further, for he was their ruler as well as England's. For another, they had spent all the money they had raised for this invasion. Nevertheless, they knew they had the advantage in the negotiations.

The stubborn King was still determined to force the ways of the Church of England upon Scotland. He gained time when the Scottish negotiators agreed to a truce of two months. In the meantime the peace discussions were to be transferred to London. But the canny Scots insisted on keeping their army in Northumberland and Durham, just in case they did not gain what they sought. The two counties had to subsist the soldiers at a cost of £850 a day.

So ended the Second Bishops' War. The King was hopeful now, as he returned to London to await the opening of the new Parliament. He had no idea that it would afflict him with troubles such as he had never known before, or that he would not live to see the end of this, the famous Long Parliament.

12

Strafford

The Long Parliament opened on November 3, 1640. Discontent which had smoldered in the hearts of the King's opponents for eleven years had had no time to leap into flame during the Short Parliament. Now this one was ready to go on the rampage.

The King made only a short speech at the first session. He asked Parliament to join him in driving the Scots out of England. First of all, without delay, it must vote the money to maintain the English army. But the House of Commons showed no enthusiasm. Its grievances must come first. Most important of all, it was resolved to bring the King's "evil councillors," as it called them, to justice and get rid of them.

John Pym was waiting for the proper moment to bring up something he had been planning with great care, but he did not begin it himself. On November 11 a member of the House of Commons rose and delivered a violent attack upon Strafford. This set the stage for Pym to destroy him, and it was perfectly timed.

Strafford had not returned to London for the opening

session of Parliament. He had been enjoying a well-earned
vacation on his Yorkshire estate. But he scented trouble for
himself with the new Parliament, and before leaving for London he wrote a friend: "I am tomorrow for London, where
more dangers beset, I believe, than any man ever went out
of Yorkshire. It is not to be believed how great the malice
is, and how intent they are about it."

The people blamed Strafford for the fiasco of the Second Bishops' War. Some of his enemies in Parliament dubbed
him "Black Tom Tyrant." Its Puritan leaders wrongly believed he was plotting to return England to the Catholic
Church. And since he was the King's most able and loyal
supporter, they saw him as the chief obstacle to their seizure
of the royal power, which now seemed within their grasp.

Strafford had just arrived from Yorkshire and would
be coming to assume his seat in the House of Lords. Pym
struck before the earl or the King had a chance to take
countermeasures. In the House of Commons he announced,
"I have a matter of the highest importance to lay before the
House. I move that it be cleared of all strangers, the doors
locked and the keys put on the table." This done, he de-
nounced Strafford and demanded his impeachment.

Pym wrought the House of Commons to such a pitch
that it swiftly approved the accusation against Strafford. Then
he went himself to the House of Lords.

He stood before the peers in his Puritan dress of sombre
black, relieved only by a broad white collar, a chunky man
with a curled mustache, pointed beard and small, shrewd
eyes. "I do here, in the name of the Commons," he said,
"accuse Thomas Wentworth, Earl of Strafford, of high treason, and they have commanded me further to desire that he
may be forthwith committed to prison."

Strafford was conferring with the King before going to

the Lords. Word of what was going on in the House of Commons leaked out and reached Whitehall Palace.

"I will go and look my accusers in the face," he said, and strode in fury to the House of Lords. He came in just as Pym was making his accusation. He was ordered to retire outside.

The House of Lords was no longer the bulwark of the King which it had been in the early days of his reign. It obeyed Pym's demand. Strafford was called back and ordered to kneel before the peers.

"I request permission to speak," he said.

"No!" came a mighty shout. Then Black Rod took his sword from him and escorted him out of the chamber.

The news was already sizzling up and down the streets of London. A crowd had gathered outside the House of Lords.

"What is the matter?" asked a bystander as Strafford was led away to the Tower of London.

Strafford forced a smile to his haughty countenance. "A small matter, I warrant you," he replied.

"Aye," sneered the onlooker, "high treason is indeed a small matter."

Now, as never before in the King's reign, the House of Commons was feeling its power. While Strafford awaited his trial, the Commons voted to release Prynne, Burton and Bastwick from prison. The three who had lost their ears in the pillory returned to London in triumph, cheered by a multitude.

Next, the Commons declared that ship money was an illegal tax. This laid the foundation for the impeachment of the King's judges who had found it legal, including the luckless Lord Keeper of the House of Lords, John Finch, who as a judge had sentenced John Hampden for refusing to pay. A fortnight later Finch was impeached, but before he could be tried he fled by night to a ship which carried him to safety in Holland.

Not the least of Parliament's grievances was the King's power to dissolve it whenever he pleased. Now it made sure that never again should eleven years elapse between Parliaments. The Triennial Bill, providing that the King must summon one at least every three years, was introduced.

The King could say very little to all this bold defiance of his royal prerogatives if he were to carry out his cherished plan to vanquish the Scots, for he was still in desperate need of money. He summoned both Houses of Parliament to Whitehall. If they would vote him the subsidies he needed, he told them, he was prepared to make certain concessions. The hated "innovations" in the Church of England should be abolished. The courts of justice should obey the law in carrying out their duties. Any source of royal revenue which was illegal should be abandoned.

The House of Commons was suspicious of these promises. Too often in the past the King had found ways of getting around them. It decided first to trade a subsidy of £140,000 for his approval of the Triennial Bill. Both measures were passed and sent to Charles the same day. Much as he abhorred the idea of giving up his privilege of calling Parliaments at will, he signed both bills.

The power to which the Puritans had risen was shown when the House of Commons took up a petition that all bishoprics of the Church of England be abolished. But the crafty Pym saw that this might cost the Puritans the support of Church of England legislators. Instead he induced the Commons to impeach the highest prelate of the church, Archbishop Laud, who was unpopular with almost everyone. He was an old man now, in frail health, and his usual arrogance deserted him as he tottered off to the Tower.

And now all was ready for Strafford's trial. Only the House of Commons could bring an impeachment against him, but only the House of Lords could decide his fate. And although there was now much opposition to the King among the Lords, Strafford was a peer like themselves. They would be reluctant to send him to his death.

The trial began on March 22, 1641, in Westminster Hall. Every seat in the tiers of benches forming the spectators' section in the great chamber was taken, and the best seats, reserved for the House of Commons, were also filled. The galleries, set aside for the King's court, were packed with titled ladies.

The peers sat on the opposite side, around a throne erected on a platform. Below it was the seat occupied by the presiding officer of the Lords. Before him sat the judges, who would take no part in the trial except to be consulted on points of law. A bar separated this section from a desk where the prisoner sat. To one side were seats for his lawyers, to the other a witness box.

The King did not sit on the throne, since by custom Parliament did no business while he occupied it. He and Queen Henrietta took seats in a section screened from view by a lattice. With an impatient gesture, the King tore down the barrier so he could see better.

There were seven charges against Strafford: that he had tried to overthrow the governments of England and Ireland to substitute tyrannical ones in their places, advised the King to use military force to compel his subjects to submit to this tyranny, taken for his own use huge sums of money supposed to be used to pay the army, encouraged the Catholics

The Trial of Strafford

in order to gain their support for his evil designs, stirred up enmity between England and Scotland, betrayed Conway into the disastrous English defeat at Newburn and tried to destroy the rights of Parliament.

These things, it was charged, were treason, and for them Strafford must pay with his life.

While John Pym was reading the charges, Strafford sat quietly at his desk. He was no longer the haughty figure London knew well. For some time he had been in poor health from severe attacks of the gout. The weeks in the Tower had told on him too. Those in Westminster Hall saw a stooped, aging man whose black hair and beard were streaked with gray. He sat huddled in a long coat for warmth, and on his head, to ward off drafts, he wore a close-fitting, fur-lined cap.

Yet when he rose to reply to Pym, he was the old Strafford. His eyes, with their alert, keen look, flashed with fire. Like a wolf at bay, he fought desperately against the hounds who had hunted him down.

By using facts proved by records, Strafford pinned down witnesses who tried to use unsupported evidence against him. By the end of the first week he had a definite advantage over his accusers, and the House of Commons, the Lords and the spectators knew it.

To Pym and his associates, Strafford's conviction was all-important. In the background behind this trial a veritable witches' cauldron of black intrigue was bubbling. And it was a game in which the Scots held some very high cards.

The Puritan leaders were doing their best to make friends with the Scots, whose aid would be vital if a civil war between the King and Parliament broke out. Through the efforts of Pym and the others, Parliament had sent £10,000 to the Scottish army. Since this money had originally been intended for the English army, there was much resentment among its officers. Some of them began to plot a revolt against Parliament.

The plan was for the English army to the north to march against London and seize the Tower. With that fortress in its possession, it would control the city. Meanwhile, the 9000 troops Strafford had raised in Ireland would land at Portsmouth and march north. The rebels would oust Parliament, and Charles would once more rule with all the power of the divine right of kings.

When the King was told of the scheme, he said, "All these ways are vain and foolish, and I will think no more of them." But he did not overlook the importance of the army's support. He managed to send it some money. At the same time, he too was trying to win the goodwill of the Scots.

One of the army plotters had become disgruntled when he was told he was not to command the march on London as he had expected. He revealed the plot to one of the Puritan members of the House of Commons, who promptly told Pym.

An attack of this kind was what Pym feared most, especially if it were led by Strafford. "He must not be acquitted," he told the other Puritan leaders. "We must find some way to make sure he dies."

"Let us bring a bill of attainder against him," one of his friends suggested.

A bill of attainder had occasionally been used by English Parliaments before Charles I's reign to get rid of unpopular royal ministers. It was a vicious method, for it denied an accused person a free man's right to a trial. The framers of the Constitution of the United States wisely included a clause which specifically forbids bills of attainder.

But for the Puritan leaders' purposes it was a monstrously clever idea. Under a bill of attainder, Parliament simply passed such a bill declaring the accused person guilty. And the House of Commons as well as the Lords would have a hand in it.

It was necessary for the King to approve a bill of attainder, but Pym was confident that if it were passed by Parliament, public opinion against Strafford would force Charles to agree. Nevertheless, he did not want to use it if it could be avoided. They would wait, he told his colleagues, and see what happened as the trial progressed.

Pym had a plan he hoped would make a bill of attainder unnecessary. He put Sir Harry Vane, the King's Secretary of State, on the witness stand. Vane should have been on the King's side, but he did not like Strafford and feared the Puritans' vengeance if he did not do as Pym wished.

Sir Harry had been at a session of the Privy Council after the Short Parliament was dissolved. He had made notes of what Strafford had said in advising the King to send an army against the Scots.

This was what Strafford had added, according to Vane: "Your Majesty, having tried all ways, and being refused, in this case of extreme necessity and for the safety of your kingdom you are absolved from all rules of government. You have an army in Ireland; you may employ it to reduce this kingdom."

". . . this kingdom . . ." Did it mean Scotland—or *England?* Pym hoped to convince the Lords that Strafford had indeed advised the King to use the Irish army to subdue England.

But Strafford skillfully pried the jaws of this trap apart. He introduced witnesses to prove the plan had been to land the Irish army near Ayr, on the western coast of Scotland.

Other members of the Privy Council declared that Strafford had not proposed to bring the Irish army to England.

Strafford himself reminded the peers that what had happened to him could befall any of them who might serve on the Privy Council, although its proceedings were supposed to be kept secret. "I never thought before that an opinion should make a traitor," he warned. "If I am to be judged one for honestly delivering an opinion under oath of secrecy, I do not think any wise and noble persons will hereafter upon such perilous and unsafe terms venture to be a councillor to the King."

The peers were greatly impressed, and Pym saw that he had lost. Yet he still had the House of Commons with him. The important support of the people of London too, for it made no difference to them that Strafford had disproved Vane's charge; they believed it and were enraged.

Pym had the bill of attainder introduced into the House of Commons. This defiance of the Lords' authority to judge Strafford angered them. They declared they would continue the trial and ignore the attainder. Nevertheless, the Commons passed the bill on April 21 by 204 to 59.

The King was sure now that the offended Lords would not approve it, and Strafford would be saved. But he knew he must assure them that the earl would never again hold public office. On April 23 he wrote regretfully to Strafford in the Tower and told him so.

He added, "Yet I cannot satisfy myself in honour or conscience without assuring you in the midst of your troubles that upon the word of a king you shall not suffer in life, honour or fortune." Thus did the King give his faithful servant a solemn promise that he should not die.

But Charles reckoned without the power of the people.

The crowd gathered in the Palace Yard at Westminster grew bigger each day, and its temper was ugly. It howled for Strafford's execution. In Whitehall Palace the courtiers were in a panic lest the rabble storm it.

On May 2 there was a wedding at Whitehall. Although she was not yet ten years old, Charles's oldest daughter, Princess Mary, was married to the twelve-year-old Prince William of Orange. Actually it was only a formality, and like Charles's own marriage a political arrangement by which the King hoped to gain Holland's support.

It was not a time of merrymaking, but a day of gloom, with the mob's roar from Westminster even more menacing. The King had just made a mistake so serious that his life and that of the Queen and the royal family were placed in danger.

That morning of May 2, an army officer, Captain Billingsley, appeared at the gate of the Tower of London with a hundred men. He demanded to see William Balfour, the lieutenant of the fortress-prison.

Balfour was summoned. "What do you want?" he asked.

"I have an order signed by the King, commanding you to admit me and my men," replied the officer. "His Majesty desires to make sure the prisoners will be safe from any attack by the mob."

Balfour was a Scot and no friend of the King. He knew very well that Billingsley was there to rescue Strafford and get him out of England.

"I cannot let you enter," he said. Then he sent word of what had happened to his superior, Lord Newport, the constable or commander of the Tower. Newport, who was disloyal to the King, informed the House of Commons.

When the news reached the House of Lords, the peers were shocked and indignant. By trying to take Strafford's fate out of their hands, the King had turned them against him. Now they were ready to pass the bill of attainder.

Knowing the King was in the most serious trouble of his reign, Strafford decided to sacrifice himself in devotion and loyalty to his sovereign. He released Charles from his promise. "To set your Majesty's conscience at liberty," he wrote, "I do most humbly beseech your Majesty, for protection of the evils which may happen by your refusal, to pass this bill."

On May 8 the House of Lords passed the bill of attainder. Only 48 peers voted, and of these only 11 dared to vote against it.

The King was in agony. He summoned the Privy Council, the judges at Strafford's trial and four bishops. All except the faithful Juxon, Bishop of London, urged him to sign the attainder.

"The Earl of Newport has assured Parliament he will order Strafford's execution even if you do not approve the attainder," said one of the councillors. "You can do nothing to save him, your Majesty, and you will be well advised to sign."

For hours the King wrestled with his conscience. Even though Strafford had released him from his promise, he felt that to sign the bill would be a betrayal. Yet the mob was just outside the palace now, and its roar was tigerish.

Charles called his council back. "If only my own person were in danger, I would gladly venture it to save Lord Strafford's life." He was stammering badly, and now his voice broke. He dashed tears from his eyes and managed to go on: "But seeing my wife, children and all my kingdom are concerned, I am forced to give way to it."

Then he signed the bill of attainder.

When they told Strafford, he grew pale and stared in

disbelief. Then he mumbled a verse from the Proverbs of the Old Testament: "Put not your trust in princes," and added, "—nor in the sons of men, for in them there is no salvation." In spite of his letter, he had not believed the King would forsake him.

Then he said to the prison keeper, "Pray go to Archbishop Laud and ask him to give me his blessing. I shall be most grateful if he will be at his window tomorrow when I pass by."

The archbishop was there as they led Strafford out of the Tower about noon the next day. The earl glanced toward the window and called out, "Farewell, my Lord, and God protect your innocence!" But the old man had fainted and did not hear.

On Tower Hill a mob of 200,000 bared its teeth in a savage roar. "Do not be afraid, my Lord," said Balfour. "I have a coach to carry you in safety."

"No, Master Lieutenant, I will walk," replied Strafford.

"They will tear you to pieces!" cried the keeper.

"I dare look death in the face," said Strafford, "and I hope the people too."

But they held back as he marched proudly up Tower Hill to the scaffold. He knelt there and prayed, sent last messages to his wife and children, then took off his jacket, saying, "I thank God I am not afraid of death, but do so cheerfully put off my doublet at this time as I ever did when I went to bed."

Then he spoke to the headsman: "Do not bind my eyes, for I will see it done."

It was soon done. Thus, with courage as magnificent as his devotion to the King and his country, died Thomas Wentworth, Earl of Strafford.

13

The Crisis

The great kettle of intrigue was still bubbling. It was a fight to the finish now between the King and John Pym.

With Strafford, the "evil councillor," dead, Charles regained a good deal of his popularity with the people. It worried Pym, who knew the King had not given up the struggle for his prerogatives. He struck back with a bill in Parliament to do away with still more of the royal power. Under it the court of High Commission, which Archbishop Laud had used to persecute those who violated his religious doctrines, and the iniquitous Star Chamber would be abolished.

It passed both Houses of Parliament by such large majorities that Charles dared not refuse to sign it. He could not afford to offend the peers of the House of Lords who voted for it, since he was trying with some success to stir dissension between the Lords and the Puritans of the House of Commons.

Charles was also striving to keep his control over the English army, prevent the disbanding of the army Strafford had raised in Ireland and win the Scots over to his side. If he could do so, he might move against Parliament with such a strong military force that he could regain his lost power.

The King's greatest hope was in the Scots. The three principal leaders in Scotland were the tough-minded Earl of Rothes, the Earl of Montrose and the former Lord Lorne, who had become Earl of Argyll on his father's death. All were rivals for power. Like a magician who conceals by trickery what he is really doing, Charles was attempting the feat of winning the support of all three while making each believe he was the only favoured one. Thus the King might have the aid of whoever emerged as master of Scotland.

Charles announced he would be in Edinburgh in August to open the Scottish Parliament. Pym, knowing his real purpose, tried in vain to prevent the journey. He had to be content with sending two members of the House of Lords and four from the House of Commons to Scotland as observers, a polite way of saying they were to spy on the King.

Pym then made a move he hoped would discredit the King and destroy his renewed popularity. He introduced what was known as the Grand Remonstrance into the House of Commons. It listed every unpopular action of the King since the beginning of his reign. It was designed to show he was unfit either to appoint ministers and other officials or to have control over the army. Taking away these powers was Pym's next objective.

In Scotland, meanwhile, the King tried mightily to win support. He approved bills the Scottish Parliament had passed making that country's government practically independent of royal authority. Such defiance could be dealt with later, once he had regained his power in England.

Suddenly the King found himself "hoist by his own petard"—caught in one web of intrigue while he himself was spinning another. One of the three rivals for power in Scotland, Rothes, had fallen ill and died. Argyll was now the acknowledged leader, for he had had Montrose arrested and imprisoned on suspicion of conniving against the Scottish government.

Charles had brought with him a number of former officers who were to have important posts in the army he hoped to raise against Parliament. They became friendly with some Scottish officers who were opposed to Argyll. Together they hatched a plot to kidnap and murder Argyll and the Duke of Hamilton.

Hamilton was a Scot who had been loyal to the King and had become one of his closest advisers. But lately Charles had begun to suspect that Hamilton was plotting against him. The King's disillusionment with Hamilton was known in Edinburgh.

As so often happens, one of the plotters decided his neck was in too much danger. He betrayed the scheme to Argyll, who made it public and implied that both the King and Montrose were at the bottom of it.

Whatever Charles had gained in his efforts to win over the Scots vanished like a puff of smoke in a gale. Before the Scottish Parliament, almost in tears, he denied he had known about the plot. Almost certainly he knew nothing of what was called the "Incident," which his ex-officers had devised. But that made no difference; he had lost his hope that the powerful Argyll would help him against the English Parliament.

Now another blow fell upon him. There had been some injustices under Strafford's rule in Ireland, but the good things he had done far outnumbered the bad. Best of all, he had had the strength to hold in check the unruly Irish Catholics, who had been persecuted for years, and there had been peace in the beautiful green island. But with Strafford gone, the English Parliament had forced the King to appoint two incompetent adventurers to govern Ireland. During the fall of 1641, the Catholics revolted.

Joined by the restless soldiers of Strafford's army, which had been disbanded in spite of Charles's efforts, they spread out over Ireland, burning the houses and farm buildings of the English landowners who were their oppressors, robbing and murdering. Before it was over, about 5000 English had been slaughtered and 5000 more had perished of starvation or exposure when their estates were lost to them.

In England the Puritans seized eagerly on the stories of atrocities which came out of Ireland. They circulated a report that 100,000 had died. Who was responsible? Who but the King and his papist wife, who had stirred the Catholics to revolt? So said the Puritans.

Protestant England was enraged. Once more Charles's popularity waned. Until then his friends in Parliament had been increasing. London was calling them "Cavaliers," a term for a gaily dressed, long-haired gentleman of the period, in contrast to the soberly clad Puritans, who became known as "Roundheads" because of their close-cropped hair. Now Pym and his followers were regaining power.

It was not true that the King had fomented the Irish rebellion. He wanted to put it down promptly, but since he was being blamed for it the Puritans were perfectly willing to have it go on.

Back in England and confronted with this problem, Charles faced another of critical importance—the Grand Remonstrance. If it were passed, Pym's next move would be to have Parliament take over control of the army. That must not happen.

There was new trouble over the English Catholics too.

Queen Henrietta had never given up her attempts to gain tolerance for them. Through her powerful influence over the King, the Penal Laws against them had not been strictly enforced. One of these laws forbade Catholic priests to remain in England under pain of death. Now the Puritans began enforcing them.

A number of priests were seized and imprisoned. One, William Ward, who was seventy-six years old, was condemned, hanged and quartered, and his heart was publicly burned. The Puritans hated him especially because he had been converted from a Protestant.

Much of this Puritan resentment was directed against the Queen, who had kept priests and other Catholic advisers about her. One, a French diplomat, became so deeply involved in intrigue that the King was forced to send him home.

There was another French troublemaker at the English court. Dowager Queen Marie de' Medici of France, widow of the great King Henry IV, had come to visit her daughter. She too was a great intriguer and aided Henrietta's efforts in behalf of the Catholics. The people's anger against her became so intense that Charles had to tell Henrietta her mother must return to France.

The old French Queen left, but now Henrietta herself was in danger. The King had already decided on drastic action against Pym and the other Puritan leaders if the Grand Remonstrance were passed. His resolution was strengthened when he heard a rumour that they planned to impeach and try Henrietta for treason.

The Grand Remonstrance did pass the House of Commons by a vote of 159 to 148. The King then began his preparations for revenge in great secrecy with a few of his most trusted advisers.

On January 3, 1642, the King's attorney general appeared in the House of Lords. He read an impeachment for high treason against five members of the House of Commons—John Pym, John Hampden, Denzil Holles, Sir Arthur Hazelrigg and William Strode—and one member of the House of Lords, Edward Montague, Viscount Mandeville.

The charges were that they were traitors who had tried to overthrow the laws and government of England, depriving the King of his rightful power, to establish tyranny over the people of England, to influence the army to disobey the King's commands, to induce a foreign power (Scotland) to invade England and to force Parliament to join them in their traitorous plans, and that they had conspired to make war against the King.

Then Charles sent a sergeant-at-arms to the House of Commons with orders to arrest its five accused members. This was an affront to the House of Lords, whose custom it was to order the arrest of those it would try under an impeachment. The House of Commons refused to allow the officer to make the arrests. It would appoint a committee, the King was told, to decide whether its five members should be punished.

That evening at Whitehall, the King held a conference with his advisers. Queen Henrietta was also present.

"Your Majesty, I humbly urge you to go in person to the House of Commons and arrest the five members," said Lord George Rigby.

"Yes, Charles, you must do so!" the Queen implored.

The King could not make up his mind. This was the most crucial decision of his reign. There must be no wrong move. He decided to wait until morning.

The delay was fatal. Queen Henrietta was no exception

to the old saying that a woman cannot keep a secret. She whispered what was afoot to her most intimate English friend, Lucy Percy, Countess of Carlisle, who promptly blabbed it to Robert Devereux, the Earl of Essex, one of Pym's best friends.

The next morning the King still could not decide. At last Henrietta stomped into his study. She was pale and quivering with rage.

"Go, you coward!" she cried. "Pull those rogues out by the ears or you will never see my face again!"

And with that the King of England slunk downstairs and entered a coach at the palace door. With him was the young Elector Palatinate, who was in England in the vain hope that Charles might help him regain his lost kingdom. Three or four hundred armed men followed the coach to Westminster.

They formed protecting walls of two ranks between which the King strode through Westminster Hall. At the stairs leading to the second floor of adjoining St. Stephen's Chapel, meeting place of the House of Commons, he signalled them to remain outside. Nevertheless, about eighty of them followed him up to the lobby of the Commons, but before Charles entered the chamber he called out: "On your lives, remain outside!"

They obeyed, but his friend Robert Kerr, the Earl of Roseburgh, leaned against the door, holding it open. Thus the members of the Commons inside could see that the guards were armed with swords and pistols, ready to fight to the death to defend the King.

Charles made his entrance with courtesy. He first sent in word to the Commons that he had come. Then he stepped inside. It was the first time a king of England had ever entered there. Always before, a ruler had summoned the Commons to come to him. It was an indication of the power the sovereign had lost, power never to be regained.

This upper chamber of St. Stephen's Chapel was a gloomy place. Its windows, mounted high on the walls of sombre panelled wood, let in little light. Along each side, tiers of benches rose so steeply that the members who occupied them might have been cardboard cutouts stacked up there, looking as if a puff of wind would collapse them. The drab costumes of the many Puritans made the place seem even more dismal.

The members were polite too. They removed their high-crowned, broad-brimmed hats as the King came in.

Charles's eyes roved about as he advanced toward the Speaker's chair at the upper end of the chamber. When they fell upon the place John Pym usually occupied, he gave a start.

The seat was empty.

The King quickly regained his composure. "By your leave, Mr. Speaker," he said, "I must borrow your chair a little." As he stood in front of it his eyes swept the chamber again, seeking the other men he had come to arrest.

But the House of Commons had already been warned by Essex. When word came that the King was on his way, Pym, Hampden, Hazelrigg and Holles left. But Strode obstinately remained in his seat until another member hauled him off by the collar to join the other four at the nearby landing on the Thames. There a boat took them downstream to safety in the City.

Now the King was speaking: "Gentlemen, I am sorry for this occasion of coming unto you. Yesterday I sent a sergeant-at-arms to apprehend some that by my command were accused of high treason, whereunto I did expect obedience. No king that ever was in England was more careful of your privileges to maintain them to the uttermost of his power, yet you must know that in cases of treason no person hath a privilege."

He went on: "I am come to know if any of those persons that were accused are here." Once more he looked around, then muttered, "I do not see any of them. I think I should know them. I must have them, wherever I find them. Is Mr. Pym here?"

There was no answer.

"Is Mr. Holles here?"

When there was still silence, the King turned to William Lenthal, the Speaker. "Are any of these persons in the House? Do you see any of them? Where are they?"

Lenthal fell to his knees. "May it please your Majesty, I have neither eyes to see nor tongue to speak but as this House is pleased to direct me, whose servant I am. I humbly beg your Majesty's pardon that I cannot give any other answer to what your Majesty is pleased to demand of me."

Charles tried to appear cheerful as he replied, "Well, I see all the birds have flown. I do expect from you that you shall send them to me as soon as they return hither. If not, I will seek them myself, for their treason is foul, and one you will thank me to discover."

He turned and marched toward the door, between the high-tiered benches. Outside, those of his guard who were in the lobby grew tense in the expectation that the King would command them to disperse the disobedient House of Commons. But he gave no order, though upon his return to Whitehall he issued one for the arrest of the five accused members. It had no effect.

A few days later the King and Queen went to Hampton Court Palace outside London. For Henrietta it was the first stop on her flight from England.

On February 23 the Queen, with her daughter Princess Mary, embarked at Dover in a warship which would carry them to Holland. When Charles parted from his beloved wife, both of them burst into tears. The Queen's indiscretion in revealing the secret of the plan to arrest the five men was forgotten. Henrietta said later, "Never did he treat me for a moment with less kindness than before it happened— though I had ruined him."

As the vessel headed into the North Sea, the King mounted his horse and rode up and down the brink of the white cliffs, never taking his eyes from the white-winged ship until it disappeared over the horizon. Then he went to his palace at Greenwich, on the Thames below London, to begin his preparations for a civil war that would be his death struggle with Parliament.

14

Civil War

The King's expression was hopeful on the morning of June 14, 1645, as he gazed out over the valley near Naseby. Beyond it, on the ridge known as Mill Hill, Parliament's army was drawn up. It was as if someone had drawn a keen-edged knife across the green slope of Mill Hill, leaving a long, bleeding gash, for this New Model Army wore scarlet coats; from now on the world would know English soldiers as redcoats.

True, the scarlet-clad Parliamentary army had 14,000 men, while Charles's own Royalists were only 8000 strong. But the King's nephew, young Prince Rupert, who commanded the Cavalier army, was contemptuous of the New Model Army, which Oliver Cromwell, the Puritan leader, had raised, equipped and trained. And the King's men, drawn up just down the slope of Dust Hill, did make a splendid appearance. Some regiments wore coats of blue, others green, purple, red, white, gray. Their banners, flapping in the fresh breeze, were also of many colours; the sun struck brilliant flashes from polished breastplates, the sharp heads of pikes, the officers' swords.

The King was thinking of many things as he sat, clad in his shining, gold-coloured armour, on his magnificent Flemish charger. He knew this battle of Naseby which was about to begin could change everything, even end this grievous civil war in spite of all the adversities that had come to the Royalists—battles lost, territory yielded to the enemy and, most of all, the lack of money.

Wealthy lords from all over the kingdom had been generous with loans when Charles had declared war on Parliament and looked about for the money he needed to raise, equip and pay his army. Some had put their entire fortunes at his disposal. They had flocked to support him when he raised the royal standard at Nottingham in August, 1642, and called upon all loyal subjects to join him. And they had recruited soldiers among the tenants of their great estates.

Yet Parliament had an enormous advantage. It had controlled London from the start, since the people of the metropolis were overwhelmingly in favour of the Puritans. Because it was England's greatest port, sea trade had made it the financial and mercantile centre of the kingdom. Thus the Roundheads had had a steady flow of income for waging the war. And the other principal English seaports were also Puritan strongholds.

Charles might have shut off this trade, so profitable to Parliament, if he had controlled the navy. But most of its officers and men had turned against him. The Puritans had the warships, which might otherwise have captured or sunk the merchant ships and bombarded the ports. And Parliament also controlled the principal arsenals where ammunition, powder, cannons and other arms were made and stored.

Although three-quarters of the nobles in the House of

Lords had remained loyal to the King, many of the others had rendered services which were most valuable to the Roundheads and disastrous to the Cavalier cause. The Puritan Earl of Essex, for one, had become commander in chief of the Parliamentary army, and his cousin, the Earl of Warwick, a real sea dog, commanded the navy.

Nevertheless, for a time things had gone well for the King's side. Now, as he was poised for what might well be the decisive battle of the Civil War, Charles's thoughts went back to the first important one.

Edgehill. Rupert had commanded there as he would do today at Naseby. At this moment the King could see him down the slope of Dust Hill, mounted on his splendid horse and wearing the red cloak of a general. He was riding along the ranks of the cavalry on the Royalist army's right wing, which he would lead in the fight.

He was a brilliant young man, this brother of the Elector Palatinate, and feared by the enemy. Whenever Parliament's army found itself facing Rupert's men, terrified whispers flew among the superstitious Roundhead soldiers:

"Marry, they say 'e's in league with the Devil, for 'e's been seen in three different places at once!"

"Aye, and no bullet can touch 'im!"

"Swifter nor the wind, 'e is, when 'e rides in a charge, a-butchering with 'is great sword!"

The Royalist soldiers loved and respected Rupert. Their affections extended even to the white dog which followed him everywhere. Looking down the slope of Dust Hill, Charles could see the animal trailing at the heels of the prince's mount. A faint smile turned up the corners of the King's mouth as he recalled how the men had christened the dog "Sergeant-Major-General Boy" in a ceremony with full military honours.

Already, at 25, Rupert was a veteran of the fighting in Germany, an expert in artillery, fortifications and siege warfare, fearless and quick at making decisions and carrying them out. He had won several important victories. But he was inclined to be impetuous, too impetuous sometimes. There flashed into the King's mind a picture of the action at Edgehill.

The two armies had been equally matched on that battlefield in Warwickshire. Nevertheless, the Royalist officers had been confident of a smashing victory over the rabble Essex had assembled, sure many of his officers would desert once they heard the King himself was there.

And it had happened. When the Royalist cavalry charged the enemy, traitorous cavalry officers and their men on the Puritan left wing had wheeled and joined the King's riders. It threw the whole left side of the Puritan line into confusion; the rest of the cavalry and the infantry there turned and fled.

The entire force of the King's horsemen, led by Rupert, gave chase all the way to the neighbouring village of Kineton. On the battlefield of Edgehill, the Royalist infantry was left without cavalry protection. The Puritans still had two mounted regiments on the field. Slashing with their swords, they had cut much of the Cavalier infantry to pieces. By the time Rupert and his horsemen returned, night was falling and both sides drew off.

The Royalists had gained an advantage in this drawn battle, for Essex retreated to Warwick, leaving the road to London open. The King's army captured Banbury and Oxford, though they found London too strongly fortified to risk an assault. Thus the Puritans had gained the real advantage, since but for Rupert's mistake the Roundhead army might have been annihilated and the Civil War ended.

London had to be taken, however, if the war were to be won. The King and his generals planned a three-pronged advance upon the city. From the southwest an army raised in Cornwall and Devon would march. Another from York-shire would come down the Great North Road. The King, with his main army, would strike through the valley of the Thames. On their way the three forces would capture the fortified towns held by the Puritans.

But the men from Cornwall and Devon feared that their homes and families would be devastated by the Pu-ritans, who occupied the stronghold of Plymouth on the Devon coast. They turned back and laid siege to it. Mean-while, the northern army was checked by a Puritan one in southern Yorkshire. And although the King's army routed the Roundheads in a battle at Newbury, the Puritans escaped to London, which remained safely in their hands.

Nevertheless, the King held most of the north, west and southwest of England at the end of 1643. If his armies kept relentlessly hammering at the Parliamentary forces, it seemed that another year should give the Royalists victory. Then came a stunning blow—Scotland.

The King had hoped to gain the Scots' support, but the canny Earl of Argyll, now the country's real ruler, felt he could gain more by an alliance with the English Parliament. Well aware of his strong position when it came to bargain-ing, he offered Pym a treaty on some very stringent terms.

Knowing the alliance was the Puritans' best hope of winning the Civil War, Pym accepted. Under the treaty, the religion of England would become Presbyterian. The Scots would send an army of 20,000 into England. Its expenses were to be paid by Parliament at £150,000 a month. And when a peace treaty was signed with the Royalists, the Scots' demands were to be included.

Pym was ill of a wasting disease, yet he strove mightily to raise the stupendous sum needed to pay the Scots. As he goaded Parliament into voting backbreaking new taxes, he often fainted.

In January, 1644, the Scottish army under Alexander Leslie, Earl of Leven, crossed the Tweed and entered England. The combined Royalist armies of Prince Rupert and the Earl of Newcastle collided with the Scots, joined by a Parliamentary army led by Oliver Cromwell, on lonely Marston Moor in Yorkshire. The Royalists had only 15,000 men against the enemy's 25,000. The Cavaliers were crushed and 4000 of them slain, while the other side lost few. And most of the north of England was lost to the King.

Then something had happened which raised the King's hopes immeasurably. The Earl of Montrose, who had been released from prison, was bent on mischief which boded ill for his successful rival, Argyll.

In the wild mountains of northern Scotland the Highlanders were Catholic. They had ignored the Covenant and continued to worship in their own faith; and the Lowlanders dared not interfere. Now Montrose had gone into the Highlands and raised an army there which was loyal to King Charles. It was aided by another royal force from Ireland.

It was an untrained horde, ragged, many of them barefoot, but there were no more rugged fighting men in all Britain than these clansmen. Armed with the great double-edged swords known as claymores, pikes, knives and clubs, they were now running rampant through Scotland. They had already beaten a Lowland army twice their size and had captured Perth, Aberdeen and Dundee.

The alarmed Argyll had been forced to call back part of the Scottish army, which had gone to England to aid the Puritans. If Montrose continued his successful rampage, all the Scots might have to return to save their country. If that happened, Charles had no doubt his army could beat the Puritans.

Now, scanning the enemy's red line across the valley on Mill Hill, he saw some of the infantry of the Puritan left wing move still farther to the left. But he did not see that these 1000 picked dragoons were being placed behind a double row of hedge. From there they could rake the cavalry of the Royalist right wing along their front if they charged.

Nor did the King know that early that morning, Oliver Cromwell, with 600 cavalry, had ridden into the enemy camp. The Puritan army was commanded by Sir Thomas Fairfax, but Cromwell, as lieutenant general, was its military genius. When he reached the camp the whole army had given a mighty shout. With Cromwell among them, the soldiers were sure of victory.

As he waited for the first move that would hurl both armies into the tumult of battle, Charles's thoughts turned to his family. Henrietta—what a rock of loyalty, strength and tireless energy she had been to him.

In Holland she had worked ceaselessly to obtain money, arms and men for the Royalist cause. When that failed she had pawned the priceless jewels with which she had fled from England. They had brought £180,000.

Then, with a convoy of ships loaded with the arms she had bought with the money, she had sailed for England early in 1643. The vessels had been forced back to Holland in a fearful storm, but she had set out again, eluded the Parliamentary navy and landed near Newcastle.

It had been several months before Henrietta had been able to join her husband. Charles's eye glowed with pride as he saw her again when he had ridden out from Oxford to meet her—his dark-eyed, valiant little Queen, riding at the head of the small army she had brought from York. Their reunion had been joyful, the old days of quarrelling long forgotten.

Gloom creased Charles's forehead as he thought of her now, far away from him. They had been together almost a year at Oxford, the seat of the King's government. Then Henrietta, expecting another child, had gone to Devon, Royalist territory, where she would be safer. At Exeter, on June 16, 1644, she had given birth to a daughter, the Princess Henrietta.

Then the Earl of Essex, leading a Puritan army, had advanced toward Exeter, hoping to capture the Queen. Ill and exhausted, she had been forced to flee to France. Though there was no thought in the King's mind that he would never see her again, he missed her terribly.

His children had become far closer to his heart in these perilous times. He worried most about ten-year-old Princess Elizabeth and Prince Henry, the Duke of Gloucester, who was nearly five. At the beginning of the war both had fallen into the hands of Parliament. Charles had assurances that they were safe and well cared for, but they could be used as hostages. Suppose the Puritans threatened their lives in order to force him to capitulate?

Mary was in Holland with her young husband, the Prince of Orange. Of the two older boys, eleven-year-old James, Duke of York, was at Oxford in the care of the city's governor. Charles, fifteen, the heir to the throne, was also safe, far to the west, at Bath.

Sadly, the King shook his head. When would all the family be reunited? It would depend, he thought, upon Montrose in Scotland and this battle today at Naseby.

Three years of war—many of his loyal friends had died in the fighting. The staunchest of all his supporters, save for

Strafford, had died too, though not in battle. William Laud had continued to languish in prison after Strafford's execution, but the Puritans had not forgotten him.

Earless William Prynne had dug up flimsy "proof" that the archbishop was in league with the Pope. The House of Lords refused to try him for treason on such trivial evidence, so the House of Commons, as it had done in Strafford's case, drew up a bill of attainder, passed it and sentenced Laud to death. The hoary old man of seventy-one had tottered to the block on January 10, 1643, mumbling, "Lord, I am coming as fast as I can." Then the executioner struck off his head.

Some of the King's foes too were dead. John Hampden had been mortally wounded in battle in June, 1643, near Oxford. And Charles's archenemy John Pym was gone. In spite of his illness, he had cheated death just long enough to conclude the alliance with the Scots in November, 1643, hanging onto life with unyielding tenacity. A fortnight later he was dead.

There had been no lack of others to carry on in his place—Oliver Cromwell especially. Before the war little had been heard of this Puritan member of the House of Commons. But once hostilities had begun, he rocketed to fame as a military genius. The King had never met him. He wondered about this strange man, fanatically devoted to his Puritan religion—what was his destiny?

Fate was soon to determine his destiny on this very field of Naseby, for now the Royalist army began to move down into Broad Moor in the valley below. On Mill Hill, orange flame belched from one of the Roundhead cannon with a roar. The battle was on.

As he had done at Edgehill, Rupert led the cavalry on the Royalist right wing up the slope of Mill Hill in a charge so furious that the fire of the Roundhead troops behind the hedge could not halt them. They met the cavalry of the Puritan left head on. Two of the enemy mounted regiments and part of the infantry crumpled and fled to the rear. And again as at Edgehill, Rupert and his horsemen deserted the battlefield to pursue them.

Meanwhile, the infantry in the centre of the two opposing armies' lines met in combat. At the same time, the 2000 cavalry on the Royalist left wing began their advance up the hill. Oliver Cromwell charged them with 3600 riders. The King's horsemen were thrown back into retreat.

Cromwell sent only three of his mounted regiments to pursue them. With the rest he rode down upon the Royalist infantry.

The foot soldiers on both sides were musketeers and pikemen. Reloading the muskets of those days took a long time, and the clumsy, unwieldy weapons had to be rested on a portable stand to be fired. The pikemen, with their long poles tipped with sharp iron heads, were actually better off. But with part of the Royalist cavalry chasing the fleeing enemy regiments and the rest in retreat, the Royalist pikemen had no protection from Cromwell's charging horsemen, slashing with their sabres.

The King, seeing the danger, galloped toward the retreating cavalrymen, shouting, "Stand! Throw the enemy back!"

He was about to hurl himself into the fight when one of his aides snatched at his bridle. "Will you go to your death, your Majesty?" he demanded.

As Charles hesitated, trying to decide between attempting to rally the fleeing cavalry and the need of not risking his life, someone shouted, "March to the right!" The Royalist cavalry wheeled and galloped that way, taking the King with them in their mad rush.

Now Cromwell's swordsmen rode into the midst of the savage fight between the infantry of the two armies. Before such an overwhelming phalanx of riders, the Royalist foot soldiers were helpless, in danger of being cut to pieces. One after another, the regiments flung down their arms and surrendered. One regiment did stand its ground and was annihilated.

Too late, Rupert returned from his chase. Further resistance was futile, for nothing was left of the Royalist army but the cavalry. It was ordered to retreat, pursued by the Puritan horsemen, slaughtering as they rode. Fairfax's army took 5000 prisoners, including 500 officers, and captured all of the Royalists' arms and baggage.

Although the King must have known he had lost the Civil War, he did not give up. There was still his army in Yorkshire. If Montrose could conquer Scotland . . .

For a time it seemed that he might do so and save England for the King as he continued to rout the Covenanters. When Glasgow and Edinburgh surrendered to him he was virtually the master of Scotland and could think of going to help Charles.

But Montrose's clansmen were sated with booty. Hordes of them deserted and went home to their mountains with their loot. Then, at Philipspaugh, in the Lowlands, Montrose and the 700 troops he had left were caught off guard by a Covenanter army three times as large. His force was destroyed, and he barely escaped with his life.

Meanwhile, in England, castle after castle, town after town was taken by the Puritans. The Royalist army which remained in the north dwindled until there was little of it left. By the spring of 1646 all of England except for a few small pockets of territory was held by the Puritans.

Oxford was one of these little islands. The King was

there in this last desperate refuge. Though he still hoped for some miracle, he gave thought to preserving the life of his oldest son, Charles, the heir to the throne. Late in 1645 the prince had withdrawn into Cornwall, still Royalist territory. But the Puritan commander in chief had advanced into that southwesternmost part of England, and young Charles was taken by sea to the little dots in the Atlantic off the tip of the kingdom known as the Scilly Isles. Still he was not safe, so he fled to the English island of Jersey, not far off the coast of France.

While the King remained at Oxford, he learned of a rift between the Puritans and the Scots. With victory in their grasp, the Roundheads could afford to be less accommodating to their allies. And the Scots were disgruntled because their army had not been paid as promised by the English Parliament.

One of Charles's weaknesses was that he too often engaged in the dangerous practice of intriguing with both sides at the same time. He did so now, offering to come to London to negotiate terms with Parliament, while at the same time he sent his agent Jean de Montreuil to treat with the Scots.

The Puritans, thinking they had the King trapped, were closing in on Oxford. But in the darkness at three o'clock in the morning of April 27, 1646, the governor of Oxford opened a gate in the city walls and let out the King, one of his chaplains, a faithful aide and a servant. Perhaps Charles thought ruefully of his merry escapade with Buckingham to Spain, for he was also disguised now, wearing the clothes of a countryman and a false beard, with his long hair cropped short.

They went toward London first, for the King still hoped for a message inviting him to come. When none reached him, the party turned northward. There was a chance, too, that

Montreuil might send word that he would be welcomed in Scotland.

The journey was dangerous, for by now the Puritans were hunting everywhere for him. The party travelled only at night. Several times the King was almost recognized by suspicious landlords and servants at the inns along the road.

The chaplain, Michael Hudson, had been sent ahead to find Montreuil and learn what the Scots might offer. When he returned, he reported, "The Scots will receive you with safety and honour, your Majesty. They will not force you to do aught against your conscience."

"Does Montreuil have the promise in writing?" asked the King.

"No your Majesty, they refuse to put it to paper."

It was not much, especially since the King distrusted Argyll. But he had little choice; if he did not accept the invitation, he would surely be tracked to earth by the Puritan hounds so hot on the scent.

At six in the morning of May 5, the King and his companions reached Southwell in Nottinghamshire. There, at the Saracen's Head Inn, where Montreuil was waiting, Charles surrendered to commissioners the Scots had sent there. He did not know it, but he had walked into a trap from which he would never escape.

15

The Captive

The Scots received their royal prisoner with chilly politeness. They knew the importance of what had befallen them, and they were going to use it to the fullest advantage.

They were disgruntled with the English Parliament. Only a small part of the money promised them for the support of their army had been paid. As for the agreement to establish the Presbyterian Church in England, it was proceeding so slowly that the Scots were suspicious.

With the King in their possession they were ready to trade with whichever side offered them the most. If Charles met their demands they would help him regain the throne. If not, they would see what the English would give in exchange for him.

Charles was all too familiar with the terms they offered him. He was to sign the Covenant and allow establishment of the Presbyterian Church in England and Ireland. These things his conscience would not let him do.

Now he began dickering with the English Parliament. It sent a delegation to Newcastle, where he had been taken.

The Great Seal of Charles I broken before the Lords and Commons on 11 August 1646

Although he was a prisoner, he was not treated like one, but was given much freedom, and was not closely guarded.

The terms the delegation brought from London were even stiffer. Not only must the King agree to the Scots' demand for Presbyterianism in England, but he must yield to Parliament his royal prerogative of control over the army and navy. And he must agree that certain Royalist leaders in the Civil War be punished.

He could not accept. All he would offer was that the Presbyterian religion be established in England for three years. Then a conference would decide what should be done in the future. He felt sure that once he regained his throne he could bring the Episcopal Church back as the official one of England.

He was not worried about what might happen to him. Friends kept him informed about how the people of England felt. After four years of the Civil War they were sick of the tremendous load of taxes Parliament had put upon their backs to pay for the war.

Knowing that most of them would now welcome his return, the King was sure he could strike a bargain with Parliament; if not, then with the Scots. And he knew his captors were worried lest Parliament, having won the war, would break its promises, send a Roundhead army to drive the Scots out of northern England and then invade and subdue Scotland.

The wary Scots then began to haggle with the English. At last Parliament agreed to pay them a large part of the money it had promised. When the King heard of it, he was worried for the first time. He began to plot an escape to the Continent of Europe, where Henrietta might help him raise an army to invade England.

But the Scots learned of the plan. From then on, Charles

was a real prisoner. Sentries were posted outside his quarters in Newcastle to watch him day and night.

On January 26, 1647, a delegation from Parliament arrived at Newcastle. "The House of Commons has voted that you are to come to Holmby House in Northamptonshire until England and Scotland decide the disposition of your case," its leader told the King.

The Scots had sold him out to the English. Charles had no choice but to go along. But he was much heartened during the journey. All along the route the streets of the towns and villages were black with cheering people. There were shouts of "God bless your Majesty!" Some yelled, "Judas!" at his Parliamentary escort.

Holmby House was a mansion in the pleasant Northamptonshire countryside. It was garrisoned by about fifty Parliamentary soldiers commanded by a Colonel Graves. The King was not allowed to have his Episcopal chaplains with him, and Parliament sent some Presbyterian ministers to convince him that their religion was a proper one for England. He paid no attention to them.

He was not made to feel like a prisoner, however, though he was watched by the soldiers and Parliament's commissioners who had brought him there. During the rest of the winter he amused himself by playing cards and chess with his captors and by reading Shakespeare's plays, poetry and books on theology. When spring came, he was allowed to ride with a guard to the neighbouring village of Althorp, where there was a bowling green.

Meanwhile, all was not well in London. Although England was far from being as thoroughly Presbyterian as Scotland, there were many of that sect, and they had become powerful in Parliament. They were determined that their religion should be the only one in England. But the army was

controlled by a faction known as the Independents, composed of Puritans and members of other sects. They were
equally determined that Presbyterianism should not prevail.
The split between the two groups was bitter, and it threatened to explode into open rebellion by the army against
Parliament.

That was why, on a lovely spring day early in June, the
King's game of bowls at Althorp was suddenly interrupted.
Colonel Graves, who had gone there with him, was informed
that a large troop of cavalry was approaching. He suspected
what was afoot and instantly ordered the party back to
Holmby House.

In the early hours of the next morning, the force of
500 cavalry, commanded by Cornet George Joyce, rode
through the darkness and surrounded the mansion. Suddenly
its back door was thrown open; the riders dismounted and
swarmed inside. There the garrison welcomed them joyfully.

Colonel Graves was no longer there. Probably he had
learned that agents of the Independents had induced his
soldiers to come over to their side, for he had fled earlier
that night.

The Parliamentary commissioners were roused from bed
and confronted Joyce. "What means this?" demanded one
angrily.

"I have authority from the army to seize Colonel Graves,
that he may be tried before a council of war," the cornet
replied.

"On what charges?"

"That he plotted to convey the King to London without
directions from the Parliament."

Actually, Oliver Cromwell had sent Joyce to kidnap the
King. Cromwell felt that with Charles in the hands of the

army, its power against Parliament would be increased immeasurably.

Joyce made no further move until late that day, when he heard a rumour that some soldiers were in the vicinity to rescue the King. He went at once to the royal chamber. The commissioners tried to block the way, but Charles overheard the uproar outside. "Let him come in," he ordered.

Joyce spoke respectfully: "I have come for the good of your Majesty and the kingdom. Will you accompany me to a safer place?"

"Will you promise to do no harm to my person, force me to do nothing against my conscience and allow my servants to go with me?"

"It is agreed, your Majesty."

The King was still a little suspicious when he came out of Holmby House the next morning, ready for his journey. The sight of 500 armed horsemen drawn up on the lawn was foreboding.

"What commission do you have to secure my person?" he asked. "Have you nothing in writing from your general, Sir Thomas Fairfax?"

Joyce pointed to the cavalry. "Here is my commission —behind me."

The King smiled. "It is as fair and well written a commission as I have ever seen."

Parliament's commissioners protested loudly, but it did them no good. Joyce and his riders took the King to Newmarket in Cambridgeshire.

Nevertheless, Charles's spirits were good. Here too the villagers welcomed him joyfully. And soon afterward the Earl of Argyll offered to send a Scottish army to invade England and restore him to the throne if he would agree to somewhat milder terms than before. Although he refused, since the price would still be Presbyterianism for England, he was hopeful that something could be worked out with the Scots.

At the same time, as usual, he was trying to deal with the other side. About a month after coming to Newmarket, he was moved to Caversham, across the Thames from Windsor Castle. Here he had an interview with Oliver Cromwell.

Cromwell felt the wisest course would be to restore Charles to his throne, but as a king without the prerogatives which had caused so much trouble during his reign. For his part the King, knowing of the split between Parliament and the army, hoped to use Cromwell, as leader of the army faction, to regain the crown. And while he did not intend to give up his royal privileges, he was willing to let Cromwell think he might.

Cromwell was impressed when he met the King. "He is the uprightest and most conscientious man of his three kingdoms," he told one of his friends. But at the same time he seems to have sensed that Charles was holding something back. "I wish he might be more frank," the Puritan said.

While the King was also impressed with this strange man, he did not trust him. He was convinced that Cromwell was playing the game for all the power he could get out of it.

By this time Prince Charles had left the island of Jersey, landing in France to join his mother there. But three of the King's children were still prisoners of Parliament. He was much gratified when Cromwell arranged for them to visit him. Thirteen-year-old Prince James, Duke of York, and his younger brother and sister, Prince Henry and Princess Elizabeth, were brought to Caversham for a two-day visit. Their reunion with their father was so touching that Cromwell, who was present, wept.

Soon afterward, the King was moved again. It was almost like getting home, for his new prison was his palace of Hampton Court, near London, where he and Henrietta had spent much time.

Meanwhile, he was still playing his double game with Parliament and the Scots. In October, three Scottish commissioners visited him at the palace. They offered to help him escape.

Charles decided to accept. They were to have a relay of swift horses ready at nearby Bishop's Sutton. On November 11 all was ready for the attempt. That date was chosen because it was a Thursday, a day when the King was in the habit of spending the evening alone in his bedchamber, writing letters before retiring. Thus the guards posted outside his room through the night would not discover his absence until morning.

That evening, before the guards were set, the King stole out of the palace with three of his close advisers. For a time it seemed they would surely be recaptured, for they lost their way in the darkness and it was daylight before they reached Bishop's Sutton. But the horses were there, and no one pursued them as they galloped southwestward. They reached the coast and took refuge at the house of the Royalist Lord Southampton.

Charles planned to escape to France. He tried in vain to find someone with a vessel whom he could trust not to betray him and to take him across the English Channel. But he could not remain where he was. Already, he knew, there must be a great hue and cry as his captors sought to track him down.

Just off the coast, across the narrow strip of water called the Solent, lay the Isle of Wight. The King's companions believed that its governor, Colonel Robert Hammond, would give him refuge, for although he was Cromwell's cousin he was a moderate man. Charles was not so sure. "I will go only if he will take an oath for my safety," he said.

Hammond dared not take such an oath, but he said he would do what he could to protect the King. Charles finally decided to trust the governor. He and his party were rowed across the Solent to Newport, the island's capital. There Hammond met them and took them to Carisbrooke Castle.

This fortress, built before the Roman invasion of Britain in 55 B.C., stood near the centre of the island and was surrounded by a high wall. But, like many fortifications of little military importance, it was garrisoned only by a handful of old soldiers. Charles felt sure he could escape if need be.

He was well treated at Carisbrooke, allowed a full staff of servants and much freedom. With his companions he often rode over the island's rolling meadowlands, known as downs.

The King continued his negotiations, both with the Scots and with Cromwell's Independents. He also communicated often with Henrietta, who had never for a moment given up trying to obtain help from France in restoring her husband to the throne. At last he decided he would accept the Scots' terms.

He signed an agreement with them, promising to accept the Presbyterian religion in England for three years. After that, a final settlement of the question was to be worked out. A number of the religious sects in England were to be suppressed, but there was no mention of the Catholics.

The King knew it would be fatal to his hopes if Cromwell learned about the pact. And in some way the Puritan seems to have discovered it. One story is that his agents intercepted a letter Charles had written to Henrietta, telling her what he had done. At any rate, Cromwell suddenly turned against the King. From then on he was determined that Charles should never again sit on the throne of England.

One of the King's companions came to him one evening in great excitement. "A vessel to carry you safely to France has been located, your Majesty," he said. "A boat is ready at Newport to take you across the Solent to Southampton, where the ship is ready to sail."

The King dressed in great haste, but when he reached Newport the wind had shifted. It would have been impossible for the vessel at Southampton to sail that night. Perhaps his captors learned of the plan, for soon afterward the guard at the castle was doubled and he was allowed no more rides about the island. He was now a real prisoner.

He did not give up hope of escaping, however. Henry Firebrace, an old servant who had been allowed to come to the Isle of Wight, was able to smuggle letters between Charles and loyal friends on the mainland. They devised a new plan of escape.

The King's bedroom window looked out on an inner court in which no sentries were posted. From the window he could lower himself to the top of the castle wall. From there, Firebrace was to let him down to freedom with a rope.

Firebrace shook his head when the King discussed the plan with him. There was an iron bar in the middle of the casement window. "You will never be able to squeeze through, your Majesty," said the servant. "We must somehow cut the bar and remove it."

"No," replied the King, "I am sure I can get through easily."

"Quite so, your Majesty," said Firebrace, who would not have thought of arguing even if his master had weighed 500 pounds.

The night fixed for the escape came, but just as Firebrace had feared, the King could not squeeze through the window. As had happened more than once, his own obstinacy had betrayed him.

His captors learned of the attempt, and he was moved to another room, with sentinels stationed just below its window. Nevertheless, Charles tried again. Three of the guards were bribed to help him. He was furnished with a saw to cut the bar on the window and, if that failed, nitric acid to dissolve the iron. But again the plot was frustrated when two of the guards betrayed it.

If the King could somehow get away, this was the time for it. London was seething against Cromwell's Independents. On the anniversary of Charles's succession to the throne, hundreds of bonfires blazed in the streets. A butcher was cheered lustily when he swung his cleaver in menace and threatened, "By my faith, if I could get my 'ands on that dog's-'ead 'Ammond, I'd chop 'im as small as I ever chopped a piece of beef!"

A few days later a mob of more than 3000 rampaged through Fleet Street and the Strand, bound for Whitehall to drive out one of Cromwell's regiments there. But he sent cavalry charging into them, and they dispersed.

In France, Henrietta's prospects of obtaining aid were better than they had been at any time. From Holland, eighteen-year-old Prince Charles put to sea with a fleet, planning to invade England. And in August the army the Scots had promised did invade it from the north, supported by English Presbyterians and Royalists.

Then, as so often happens, Lady Luck's smiles turned to the blackest of frowns. At the head of the New Model Army, Cromwell marched north and routed the Scots in Lancashire, capturing all their infantry. The Second Civil War, as it was called, ended soon afterward, and with it the

King's hopes in this gamble in which he had staked everything and lost.

Meanwhile, young Prince Charles's fleet was driven
back by a great storm and had to return to Holland. Queen
Henrietta's hopes too were dashed. A rebellion against the
many years of despotic rule by the French kings arose. The
rebels, known as the Fronde, seized Paris, and the government was temporarily driven out. There would be no help
for Charles from France.

On the Isle of Wight, Colonel Hammond relaxed the
King's close imprisonment. After promising he would not
escape, Charles was allowed to take lodgings in a private
house in Newport. But then Colonel Isaac Ewer was sent to
order Hammond back to the mainland.

Colonel Ewer bore another order from Cromwell. A
rumour of what it was reached the King's friends and they
urged him to escape, but he refused to break his word.

The night of November 30 was dark, cold and rainy.
The King had gone to sleep when there was a loud knocking
at the door of the house. A servant opened it, and several
of Cromwell's officers pushed him roughly aside, then charged
into Charles's bedroom.

"What is the meaning of this?" demanded the roused
but sleepy King.

"We have orders from the army to remove you to Hurst
Castle," said one of the intruders. "Get up—we have a carriage at the door."

When the King had dressed, he was hustled into the
waiting coach. One of the officers, Major Edward Rolfe,
tried to force his way into it and sit beside the prisoner.

"It's not come to that yet!" cried the King in a thunderous voice. "Get you out!" And he pushed Rolfe out, mo-

tioning to two of his friends to sit beside him. Rolfe mounted a horse and rode beside the coach, cursing the King.

They took Charles to Hurst Castle in a small boat. It stood on a long, narrow spit jutting into the Solent from the Hampshire coast. More of a blockhouse than a castle, it was gloomy and damp and had the poorest sort of accommodations. In the room where the King had his meals, candles had to be lighted at noon, even on a bright day.

There, in his lonely prison, the King remained for about three weeks. The castle's commander treated him with kindness and respect. He was allowed to take one walk a day along the rocky shore. And from his quarters he could watch ships passing by.

Late on the night of December 7, 1648, there was a great clanking outside the King's quarters. He sent his faithful servant Herbert to investigate. It was the castle drawbridge being let down over the moat.

Colonel Thomas Harrison entered the King's room. "I have been sent here with orders to conduct you to Windsor Castle," he said.

Charles was pleased. He had been often at this pleasant castle of his in the lovely valley of the Thames. It was not far from London, either. This might mean another meeting with Cromwell and a settlement.

If by now the King had any fears that all this had a more sinister meaning, they would have been lulled during his journey. Everywhere, people lined the highway. The men uncovered their heads as he passed. There were shouts of "God preserve your Majesty!" And when, on the evening of December 12, the party reached Windsor in a chill, driving rain, the people were gathered there too, drenched but joyful. There were more shouts: "God bless your Majesty and send you long to reign!"

That night the King slept in his own comfortable bed-chamber in Windsor Castle. His rest was peaceful, for he had no idea that this would be the last stop but one on his way to the scaffold.

16

The King's Trial

On the afternoon of Saturday, January 20, 1649, Charles I
of England was put on trial in the Painted Chamber of the
ancient palace of Westminster. The charge against him was
high treason, for which the penalty was death.

In the Middle Ages the Plantagenet kings had used the
Painted Chamber as the royal bedchamber. One, Henry III,
had had the walls decorated with a gorgeous pageant in
brilliant colour—kings, queens, Biblical prophets, saints and
knights in shining armour on their chargers, with the coronation of King Edward the Confessor in the centre. Time had
dimmed the colours, the paintings were now dingy, and those
parts of the panorama which were not hidden under hanging
tapestries looked a little tawdry. Nevertheless, the Painted
Chamber was impressive, especially today.

The spectators crammed into the galleries elbowed each
other for a glimpse of the King as he came in. He was all
in black—black cloak, black hat—except for the blue ribbon
of the Order of the Garter around his neck and its insignia,
a great silver star, on the cloak. Under the hat his long hair,

now very gray, fell to his shoulders. He walked quickly and steadily through the hall, without a glance to right or left, and sat down on a red velvet chair in the centre. It was placed inside a long, narrow enclosure running across the chamber, formed by two wooden barriers.

The King could look directly at the so-called commissioners who were to be his judges, and John Bradshaw, the Lord President. The commissioners were seated on tiered benches covered with red cloth at the south end of the Painted Chamber. Before them, in a chair raised on a dais, sat Bradshaw, flanked by two commissioners who were lawyers. These three men all wore the black robes of barristers or trial lawyers.

Everywhere around the sides of the hall and closely hemming the King were soldiers, some armed with sharp-pointed halberds, others with muskets. Charles's accusers were taking no chances on any attempt to rescue and spirit him away to safety.

A clerk rose and read the ordinance authorizing the trial. It would never have been enacted but for a high-handed and illegal action by Oliver Cromwell.

This had taken place before the King left Hurst Castle. On December 6, 1648, as the members of the House of Commons arrived for that day's session, they found two regiments of scarlet-clad soldiers armed with muskets drawn up before the door. They allowed 60 of the members to go in. All were members of the Independent faction. Of the rest, 160 were ordered to go home and 41 were arrested. These 201 members were of the Presbyterian faction, which held a majority in Parliament.

By this despotic action, Cromwell had made sure that the tag-end that was left of the House of Commons (they called it "the Rump") would vote to bring the King to trial.

It also prevented any move by the Presbyterian majority to come to an agreement with the King and restore him.

Although the Rump Parliament moved swiftly to approve the trial, it was done by a majority of only six votes, and the House of Lords refused to pass the ordinance. But Cromwell and the other Independent leaders simply ignored the peers' action and went ahead. The truth was, as Cromwell was well aware, that the people of England did not want King Charles killed.

During the Civil War, business of all kinds had suffered. Farmlands had lain fallow because the men who tilled them were with the armies. To make matters worse, three bad harvests had caused great suffering among the poor when the prices of food soared. And since the only government was that of Parliament, it was blamed for all these troubles. The people wanted their King back.

At no time was this more apparent than on this opening day of the trial, when the clerk called the roll of the 135 commissioners. Only 68, almost exactly half, had appeared. The reason was plain: the others feared for their lives if they sent the King to the scaffold.

When there was no response to the name of Lord Fairfax, commander in chief of the Roundhead armies, a lady in the galleries who wore a mask stood up and shrilled, "He has more wit than to be here!" It would later be known that she was Lady Fairfax.

Now John Cook, the prosecutor, leaped to his feet. He stood near the King, holding a roll of parchment. Addressing the Lord President, he said, "My Lord, in behalf of the Commons of England and all of the people thereof, I do accuse" —at that moment he swung around, glaring ferociously at the King—"Charles Stuart, here present, of high treason and high misdemeanours."

No sooner had he begun to read the charges against the King than Charles interrupted: "Hold a little."

When Cook went on reading, the King rapped him on the arm so sharply with his cane that its silver head fell off. The prosecutor paid no heed. Sternly, Bradshaw admonished Charles: "Sir, the court commands the charge to be read. If you have anything to say afterwards, you may be heard."

The King was charged with a "wicked design" to obtain unlimited and tyrannical power and to overthrow the rights and liberties of the people. He had "traitorously and maliciously" waged war against Parliament and the people it represented.

Cook concluded: "I impeach the said Charles Stuart as a tyrant, traitor and murderer, and a public and implacable enemy to the Commonwealth of England."

The King listened with a haughty, contemptuous expression. Then Bradshaw said, "Sir, you have now heard your charge. The court expects an answer."

The old stammer which had always made Charles such a poor speaker had vanished as he rose to reply. His voice was clear and forceful. But it was icy.

"I know by what power I am called hither," he began. "I would know by what authority—I mean *lawful* authority. There are many unlawful authorities in the world, thieves and robbers by the highway. Remember that I am your lawful King. I have a trust committed to me by God, and by old and lawful descent. I will not betray that trust to a new, unlawful authority. Therefore, let me know by what lawful authority I am come hither and you shall hear more of me."

Bradshaw was taken by surprise, and dismayed as well. The Lord President and others among the King's accusers and judges knew full well that he was there by no lawful authority. Cromwell had barred the lawful representatives of the people from Parliament in order to bring him to trial.

Bradshaw's rejection of the King's demand was lame: "You are being tried by the people of England, by which people you were elected King."

"England was never an elective kingdom, but a hereditary kingdom for near these thousand years," Charles replied with fine scorn. And he continued to argue that his trial was illegal. At last Bradshaw adjourned the court until Monday.

As the King left the Painted Chamber, some of Cromwell's soldiers shouted, "Justice!" A few spectators repeated it, but there were many more cries of, "God save the King!"

The judges were in a quandary. Under English law, if the King refused to plead guilty or not guilty to the charges, the prosecution could not proceed with the trial and call witnesses. The judges might declare him guilty and sentence him to death, but his treason would not have been proved. Proof was what Cromwell's faction needed to satisfy the people that Charles was indeed a traitor.

As the trial resumed, the King still refused to answer the charges. He knew his rights as an Englishman, and he also knew how important it was for them to show proof of his guilt. For two days Bradshaw badgered him without the slightest effect.

The King continued to insist that he was being tried without lawful authority. "It is not my case alone," he said. "It is the freedom and liberty of the people of England. I must justly stand for these liberties. If power without law may make law, I do not know what subject in England can be assured of his life or anything he can call his own."

Unable to stop the King's argument, Bradshaw finally ordered him removed from the courtroom and the session adjourned. But it was the same story all over again when it reconvened.

Meanwhile, there were more demonstrations for the King. All over London the people's unrest was so ominous that Bradshaw's lodgings were placed under guard, and he wore a pikeman's "pot"—a hat lined with steel to make it bullet-proof.

The judges then held a private session. If witnesses could not be heard in court, they could be examined outside it, and thirty-three of them were. Some of the newspapers printed the evidence given against the King.

With that, the judges decided to put an end to the farce in the Painted Chamber. They drafted their decision and summoned the King to hear it the following day, January 27.

The court met at ten o'clock. As soon as Charles was brought in he demanded to be allowed to speak. Bradshaw, now wearing a red robe, silenced him and then addressed the audience.

"In the name of the people of England—" he began.

"It is a lie!" came a high-pitched voice from the galleries. "Where are the people or their consents?" It was Lady Fairfax.

"Not half or a quarter of them!" shrilled another woman. "Cromwell is a traitor!"

A command rang out in the Painted Chamber, shouted by the commander of the troops there: "Present your muskets! If these slatterns try to speak again, shoot them!" But Bradshaw was so alarmed that he granted the King's demand to be heard.

"I must tell you," Charles said, "that this many a day all things have been taken away from me except that I call more dear to me than life, my conscience and my honour. Now, sir, I conceive that a hasty sentence, once passed, may sooner be repented than recalled. I desire before sentence be given that I may be heard before the Lords and Commons."

"You have already delayed justice for many days by refusing to plead," replied Bradshaw. "You will not be permitted to delay it further."

Suddenly John Downes, one of the judges, who had reluctantly consented to serve, shouted a protest: "Have we hearts of stone? Are we men?"

Others tried to silence him. Oliver Cromwell, also a judge, who was sitting in front of Downes, turned around and growled, "What ails thee? Art thou mad?"

Downes was almost in tears. "Sir, I cannot be quiet," he gasped. "I am not satisfied."

There was such pandemonium in the court that Bradshaw declared a recess. But neither the King's plea to be heard by Parliament nor John Downes's efforts in his behalf could halt the proceedings for long. Half an hour later the court reconvened.

There was utter silence in the Painted Chamber now. It was as though every soul in the packed galleries were holding his breath. The King sat like a statue of pale marble.

Then the clerk of the court rose and read the sentence of the judges: "The said Charles Stuart, as a tyrant, traitor, murderer and a public enemy, shall be put to death by the severing of his head from his body."

Charles's request to be allowed to reply was refused. Again he asked it. "Guard, withdraw your prisoner!" cried Bradshaw. As the King was led out of the courtroom, some of the soldiers laughed and blew smoke in his face; others shouted, "Justice! Execution!" When one did cry out, "God bless you, sir!" he was struck with a cane by an officer.

They took him to St. James's Palace, where he had a tormenting wait of ten days until enough signatures could be obtained for his death warrant. Only fifty-nine, less than half of the original number of judges, would do so.

The night before his execution, two of his children, thirteen-year-old Elizabeth and the eight-year-old Henry, Duke of Gloucester, were brought to him; the others had escaped to safety. As the children wept, Charles told them they must not be too sad, for he was dying gloriously for law, liberty and the true Protestant religion.

He told the prince that the Puritans might try to make him King so that they could use him for their own purposes, and that he must not yield to them as long as his older brothers were alive.

"I will sooner be torn to pieces!" the little fellow cried.

Then the King divided some jewels between them and said farewell. He spent the evening receiving religious consolation from his old friend Bishop Juxon.

Then came Charles's last night on earth, the dawn, the march to Whitehall, the agonizing delay until all was ready. And at last Charles I, King of England, stepped out upon the scaffold, spoke his last words and knelt on the block. Then, with the flash of the descending axe, for the first and last time in its history England beheaded its ruler, and with him perished the divine right of kings.

17

The Restoration

Tuesday, May 29, 1660. In London, all along the thoroughfare of the Strand, through Charing Cross and so to Whitehall Palace, the way was choked with such a mass of humanity
as the great city had never seen before. Everyone who could
ride, walk, limp or totter was there, jammed along the route,
the side streets, the windows, balconies and rooftops. The
cobblestones of the pavement could not be seen, for they
were strewn ankle-deep with flowers. Tapestries were hung
on the walls of the buildings, and many of the city's fountains
ran red with wine, pumped into them instead of water.

There was only one sombre note. Along the rooftops
one could see dark-clad figures. They were motionless, held
up by men standing beside them. And with good reason, for
they were effigies of the late Protector of the Commonwealth
of England, Oliver Cromwell. Once night fell they would be
pushed off and consumed in a thousand bonfires in the
streets.

All the bells of London had gone mad in a wild bedlam

of tinkling, pealing, jangling, clanging and deep-voiced toll-
ing. In the distance, saluting cannons thundered. But even
this discordant din was drowned out by the hoarse roar from
the throats of the multitude as the word was passed from
one to another from the arched gateway of Temple Bar to
Whitehall Palace: "He is coming!"

Coming he was—the man they had awaited all through
the morning and early afternoon. Yet there could be nothing
swift about his passage over this last mile of a journey that
had begun in Holland. Ahead of him trooped a procession
that seemed endless to the people, who had eyes only for
their idol. He would be lucky if he reached the palace by
dark.

First came a long file of gilded coaches bearing lords
and ladies, elegant in cloth of gold, silver, velvet, satin and
silk, though they might have been dressed in beggars' rags
for all anyone really cared. Behind them, squadrons of cavalry clip-clopped majestically along, the horses regal in silver
doublets. There followed a thousand infantry marching to
martial music, the sheriffs of the kingdom resplendent in
gold lace, the Lord Mayor and Aldermen of the City, the
Royal Life Guards, blaring trumpeters in black and gold and
four more regiments of cavalry.

The cavalcade's progress was made even slower by the
crowd's enthusiasm and impatience. At times it broke the
barriers of troops stationed along the footways and surged
into the street, blocking all progress until the frantic soldiers
could thrust the people back.

At last a tumult that seemed to shake the very earth
rolled gradually along the route of march. It muffled a thousand shouts: "Long live his Majesty!"—"God bless our
King!"—"Praise God, he has returned!" In the balconies,
ladies grew faint with rapture, threw kisses and tossed gar-

lands and handkerchiefs. And in the vast crowd below, men and women wept unashamed for joy.

He came riding up the Strand on his splendid charger, flanked by his brothers, James, Duke of York, and Henry, Duke of Gloucester, but the people had eyes only for their King, Charles II of England. They surveyed him with great curiosity, for when London had last seen him he was only twelve years old. Today was not only his hour of triumph but his thirtieth birthday.

The people saw a tall, very dark man in a plain dark suit. The only touches of elegance in his costume were the blue ribbon of the Order of the Garter and its insignia across his breast and the crimson plume in his hat. He was a sombre man. His rather angular figure, heavy nose and long, lean jaw were not handsome, though there was beauty in the thick, shining black hair that fell in a cascade of curls to his shoulders.

And there was beauty and more in Charles II's eyes. They were large and lustrous, softening his otherwise almost fierce expression. As he doffed his hat to left and right in response to the thunderous acclaim, his eyes held something that captivated every man, woman and child who beheld them. This was Charles II's mysterious magnetism, which was to make his people adore this returned King.

For him the way back had been bitter and filled with frustration. It had taken young Charles from France to Holland, then to Scotland, where he had accepted the Scots' terms for aiding him—acceptance of the Covenant and the Presbyterian religion for England.

There, while he waited for the promised invasion of England, the dour and stiff-backed ministers of the Kirk prayed and preached at him interminably. They admonished him sternly upon his sins and those of his father and mother, and prevented this young man who loved a good time from enjoying any sort of amusement. And at last, when the Scottish army of 26,000 men marched, Cromwell's English army of less than half that number fell upon and almost annihilated the Scots.

Charles refused to despair. He collected a new Scottish and Royalist army of 20,000 and invaded England. But again, at Worcester in the Midlands of England, Cromwell's men all but destroyed the invaders and forced Charles to flee for his life.

For six weeks he had wandered through southern England, travelling by night, never knowing when the sharp eyes of some innkeeper, villager or farmer might penetrate his disguise and set the Puritan pack snarling at his heels. At last, reaching the English Channel, Charles escaped once more to France.

For nine years he had remained on the Continent, often poverty-stricken but never giving up his efforts to recover his lost throne. Meanwhile, England became a commonwealth, governed entirely by the people's representatives in Parliament, without a House of Lords or any single ruler. But in 1653 Cromwell, backed by his army, dissolved the Long Parliament and took over the rule of England as Protector.

It was not until 1658 that hope glimmered ahead for Charles. In that year Cromwell died. His son Richard took over as Protector, but not for long. General George Monk, one of Oliver Cromwell's commanders, turned against Richard Cromwell. He marched to London with his army and restored Parliament.

Charles then sent Parliament a declaration offering concessions concerning religion, punishment of his father's enemies and other matters if he were restored to the throne. His proposals were accepted. Richard Cromwell was ousted, and the young King's return was assured.

The truth was that the people of England were sick of being ruled by a military despotism and of the crushing taxes laid upon them. They were sick too of gloomy Puritanism, which, like the Scottish Kirk, frowned upon the most innocent of amusements—and this would end under Charles II, who would be known as the Merry Monarch.

The people had gained much in the thirty-five years since Charles I had come to the throne. Yet it had been won at a terrible cost.

Years of war had devastated and impoverished England. For seven years, under the rule of a single man, the people's right to a voice in the government had been temporarily lost. True, Oliver Cromwell's rule had been good in many ways. And he had striven with some success to bring religious toleration to England. But he was a despot, and liberty-loving England did not like despotism.

Worst of all, England had killed its King. He could have been sentenced to abdicate his throne, to imprisonment, to exile. But they had murdered him. His fate is universally known to history as regicide—king-murder.

Yet rights and liberties are seldom won easily and are often achieved only through bloodshed and suffering. And at this terrible cost the people of England had gained new and important liberties. There were others still to be won, and they would be as time went on. For one thing, it would be years before all the people of England would have full freedom to worship in their chosen faith.

But one great step had been taken. Magna Carta said in effect: "The king is not above the law." This vital principle had been ignored often enough by English kings, but the

Petition of Right and the reforms passed by Parliament during the reign of Charles I ensured that it would be obeyed.

Charles I's greatest mistake was his insistence on the
royal prerogatives which violated the spirit of Magna Carta.
Because of it he died, but in time the people of England had
demanded a king again. Now they had one. Charles II would
have his battles with Parliament, and so would rulers who
followed him, but the old prerogatives which put the king
above the law were dead.

Suggested Further Readings

Of over sixty books consulted, much of the historical material for this book has come from the works of two writers. One of the great English historians was Samuel Rawson Gardiner. Three of his works were used: *History of England from the Accession of James I to the Outbreak of the Great Civil War, 1603-1642* (10 volumes); *History of the Great Civil War, 1642-1649* (4 volumes); and *History of the Commonwealth and Protectorate, 1649-1660* (4 volumes), all published by AMS Press, New York, 1965.

Another notable English historian is C. V. Wedgwood. Her trilogy was used: *The King's Peace* (1957), *The King's War* (1959), and *A Coffin for King Charles* (1964), all published by Macmillan, New York.

The serious student who wants a detailed account of this Stuart period can do no better than to consult these books. The Gardiner volumes are a complete and exhaustive study of the time: the wars, the political struggle, the principal actors in this great drama of history and conditions and life in England, Scotland and Ireland. Or for the student who wants to investigate some special aspect of the drama, these volumes are unexcelled, and the indexing is complete and well-nigh perfect.

Miss Wedgwood is also a painstaking and accurate historian. She has been praised for the clarity of her writing; I did not find her books easy reading, however, perhaps because the subject is so complex when covered in great detail, and the indexing is so bad as to make it difficult to locate the places where various subjects are covered throughout the books. But they are reliable and complete.

As for the actors, excellent biographies of Charles I, Charles II, Henrietta Maria, Oliver Cromwell, Sir Edward Coke and Buckingham are to be found in most libraries. Those of Strafford and John Pym and other opponents of Charles I are not as easily located except in the reference collections of libraries in the largest cities and colleges.

For a picture of life in Stuart England, an easy-to-read and beautifully illustrated source is Volume 2 of *A History of Everyday Things in England,* by Marjorie and C. H. B. Quennell, covering the years 1500 to 1799 (London: B. T. Batsford, Ltd., 1950). More detailed are *The Pageant of Stuart England,* by Elizabeth Burton (New York: Chas. Scribner's Sons, 1962) and *London in the Time of the Stuarts,* by Sir Walter Besant (London: Adam and Charles Black, 1903).

Index

185

6468